DEMOCRATIZATION AND WELFARE STATE DEVELOPMENT IN TAIWAN

Democratization and Welfare State Development in Taiwan

CHRISTIAN ASPALTER
Department of Social Work and Social Administration
The University of Hong Kong

Routledge
Taylor & Francis Group
LONDON AND NEW YORK

First published 2002 by Ashgate Publishing

Reissued 2019 by Routledge
2 Park Square, Milton Park, Abingdon, Oxon, OXl 4 4RN
52 Vanderbilt Avenue, New York, NY 10017

Routledge is an imprint of the Taylor & Francis Group, an informa business

A Library of Congress record exists under LC control number:

ISBN 13: 978-1-138-73181-3 (hbk)
ISBN 13: 978-1-138-73179-0 (pbk)
ISBN 13: 978-1-315-18882-9 (ebk)

Contents

List of Tables and Figures

Foreword

In reviewing the literature on Taiwan available in the 1990s, I noticed that Taiwan was not only excluded from the world community, but also to a large extent from the theoretical discourse on modernization in East Asia. Few international scholars have come to write excessively on Taiwan. Thus, the process of modernization in Taiwan never really came to the center of attention of academia in the Western world. Since it was impossible for the scope of this book to cover more than one particular colored stone in the kaleidoscope of modern Taiwan, I focused solely on the causal relationship of democratic competition of political parties and the extension of welfare state programs. Taiwan has so much to offer, especially for sociologists and political scientists who may test their theses easily at the background of a fast-running modernization process of society, a swift implementation of democracy and a mushrooming of civil society.

I am glad to have been able to live in Taiwan for such a long time, to meet and make friends with one of the friendliest peoples in the world. I had the chance to study Taiwanese people, their believes, cultures and democratic values first hand. Whenever I went out to carry out research, visiting friends or exploring the street life of Taipei, I had the chance to join numerous rallies and demonstrations. People there told me about their country, their happy and sad stories. From anti-radiation to pro-welfare demonstrations, from electioneering of Taiwan's new small and minor parties to labor protests of communist and socialist labor unions; all facets of democratizing Taiwan in the 1990s were easily accessible for foreign students like me. The Mandarin that I have learned (over the years) in various coffee shops and McDonald's restaurants helped me a great deal in discovering all the facets of modern Taiwan. Taiwan, itself was and still is one of the greatest teachers a social scientist can wish for.

The number of people I would like to thank for having had the chance of meeting them is endless, but a few I have to mention: Prof. Lin Wan-I, Prof. Chan Hou-sheng, Prof. Bai Hsiu-hsiung and Prof. Chang Zhe-ming in particular who supported me during my studies as a Ph.D. student at the Department and Graduate Institute of Sociology at Taida. I also thank numerous experts and head of departments of various government institutions, especially from the Council of Labor Affairs, the Social

Welfare Department of the Ministry of Interior, different departments of the Ministry of Economic Affairs, the Ministry of Finance, the Directorate General of Budget, Accounting and Statistics, and the Social Welfare Department of the Taipei City Government. Furthermore, I need to mention here the kind support dozens of scholars at universities and academic institutions from all over Taiwan. I have to be especially thankful to Prof. Lin Wan-I and Prof. Chan Hou-sheng from Taida, and Prof. Ku Yuen-wen and Prof. Chan Ying from National Chi Nan University in Puli for organizing social policy conferences of highest possible standards that I attended, which were very valuable for my research.

To cut short the list of those who supported me during my time in Taiwan is a pity, but not a crime. It is merely a necessity, since I don't know where to start and where to end. During the three years that I stayed in Taiwan in second half of the 1990s, I met hundreds of people who supported me. My memory is full of imposing feelings and impressions of my Taiwanese friends, who not only live for working, but who also enjoy the arts, their freedom, and their spare time to the highest degree. I wish all of them a prosperous and joyful life!

My new assignment to a teaching post in Taiwan, at Chaoyang University of Technology, will give me lots of new opportunities to meet my old friends and many new ones to come. I shall depart to Taichung soon, which gives me great pleasure. At this point, I can continue my personal task, i.e. to report and analyze Taiwan's fast-changing societal and political developments, since I look forward to the day when the world comes to understand what Taiwan is all about!

Christian Aspalter
Hon. Lecturer
Dept. of Social Work and Social Administration
The University of Hong Kong
January, 2002

1 Introduction

The book examines the relationship between democracy and welfare state construction in Taiwan; especially the impact of democratic elections on the construction and extension of the Taiwanese welfare state system. The welfare state in East Asia, these days, is drawing for the first time the attention of a great audience. The issue of globalization – and, thus, the intensified competition between worldwide production sites with different levels of social standards – emerged as a central issue in the political discourse of a great number of developed Western countries that see their high levels of social welfare expenditures as a threat to future economic development in an increasingly interdependent world economy. The notion of social dumping in the rising economies of East Asia has found its way deep into the believe system of the common people and that of government officials in the West. But, in the 1990s, the author witnessed the very same discussions about and demonstrations against the relocation of factories to cheaper production sites out of the country in Taiwan; i.e. an identical development to that in Europe. In the case of Taiwan, these were and still are above all Mainland China, Vietnam, Thailand and Malaysia. In the West, the notion goes around that it are the Tiger states that take away the masses of jobs in the globalized world economy. This is far from being true. Nowadays, however, India, Mainland China, and most countries in Southeast Asia are much more attractive for international investments since their labor force is not only abundant, but also is a great deal cheaper in comparison. The Tiger states – after years of sustained high rates of economic growth due to their booming export-driven economy – now have become also comparatively expensive with regard to production costs of labor-intensive industries.

Therefore, it is even more surprising that governments of these Tiger states do not attempt to avoid the construction of welfare state systems that either raise taxes owing to the introduction of non-contributory social insurance and assistance programs, or raise production costs directly owing to higher premiums of newly established or upgraded contributory social insurance programs. Given the particular context of globalization and the dwindling international comparative advantages of the Tiger states, the phenomenon of fast extending social security systems, i.e. social insurance and social assistance programs, as well as welfare provision in the field of education, health care and housing, poses new unanswered questions. Why are these countries taking the opposite path in welfare politics than it is expected by the vast majority in the Western world?

When looking closer to the reality of politics in these countries, i.e. when looking from an insider perspective, then we come closer to an answer to this particular question. When high levels of structural unemployment arise not only among the elder workforce, but also among young adults, then governments need to take a defensive strategy in protecting these laborers. In authoritarian countries, this needs to be done in order to avoid public unrest, such as labor protests, and to secure public peace. In democratic countries, governments will loose elections in case people are increasingly dissatisfied because of rising unemployment and job insecurity. Now, we have already hit the core of the problem governments in the East Asia are facing today, i.e. even they are not willing to raise production costs additionally (via higher taxes for social welfare and the introduction of contributory social insurance programs), they still have to respond to rising social hardships with a broad spectrum of new social welfare policies. From the mid-1980s onwards, East Asia has seen a salient, but rather silent democratic revolution, the most developed democracies in East Asia are according to the Freedom House Report (1998) Mongolia, Taiwan, South Korea, Hong Kong, Japan, and Thailand.

With the exception of Mongolia, which is a prodigious, however scarcely populated country located in between China and Russia, the other new democracies all belong to the group of most developed countries in East Asia. Thailand the latest arrival among the new democracies of East Asia, develops itself into the fifth Tiger state, due to fast economic development, especially in the vast metropolitan area of Bangkok. Singapore, though holding elections, is widely not regarded to be a full democracy, due to the all-out dominance of a single political party and the long-term absence of parliamentary opposition.

But Taiwan, South Korea, Japan and Hong Kong developed strong democracies within only one and a half decades. Taiwan and South Korea, both introduced democracy in the year 1987. In Taiwan, the Kuomintang (the KMT) struggled with the rising Democratic Progressive Party (the DPP), which first celebrated big victories in important county and city level elections. In South Korea, the ruling Democratic Justice Party lost its parliamentary majority as soon as 1988. In Japan, democratic elections did not led to significant levels of party competition in parliamentary elections and a change of the national government until 1993, when a coalition of the Social Democratic Party together with the Japan Renewal Party forced the long-term ruling Liberal Democratic Party into opposition. In Hong Kong, pro-democratic forces won landslide victories in Legislative Council elections from 1991 onward.

Moreover, these countries have all experienced long periods of high rates of economic growth which result not only in the rise of labor costs (and, thus, a decline in international comparative advantages), but also in a dramatic change of their demographic development, i.e. a rapidly aging society combined with a fast declining birthrate. The special cocktail of economic development, aging of society and the introduction of democracy sparks a revolution of its own in welfare politics.

This revolution took place most visibly in South Korea and Taiwan, the two most democratic economies of East Asia. South Korea pushed the legislation of the National Pension Insurance in 1986 and 1989; extended and reformed the National Health Insurance a great deal in the years 1988, 1989, and 1998; and established a National Employment Insurance program in 1995. Taiwan introduced a farmers' health insurance program in 1989, old-age social assistance programs beginning from 1993; set up the National Health Insurance in 1995 and a new Unemployment Insurance scheme under the umbrella of the Labor Insurance program in 1998. Japan, in the meanwhile, lags behind in the welfare development of its developed neighboring economies. The relative share of state spending in the sectors of medical care and pensions had been shrinking, but the increase in elderly population is the highest in the world. However in 1997, Japan implemented a nation-wide long-term care insurance system. Hong Kong has extended governmental welfare budgets for its social assistance programs a great deal and introduced a new contributory and fully funded provident fund scheme, the Mandatory Provident Fund (MPF), in December 2000 (cf Aspalter, 2001a; Ye, 1996; Kwon, 1998: 62-3).

Decades of research in welfare state theory have not yet led to the establishment of a convincing theory placing democratic elections and party competition, besides social movements, in the center of its explanatory theoretical construct. This book is another attempt of the author to draw the attention of welfare state theorists to the impact of democratization on welfare state development (cf Apalter, 1998; 2001b, e). This book, thus, does not only aim at showing the growth of social security programs, but also especially the electoral process that directly causes the construction of new columns of the welfare state system and the extension of existing ones. In this book, the author will not focus on the important impact of social movements on the development of the Taiwanese welfare state, or show the process of democratization itself; since this has been done elsewhere in detail (cf especially Hsiao, 2001; Schafferer, 2001). The author concentrates here exclusively on the interface between party politics, democratic elections and social policy, in order to show the causal relationship between the degree of party competition and the degree of welfare state expansion, taking the case study of Taiwan.

Electoral competition in Taiwan was introduced from the very beginning, i.e. as early as 1950; but this only in local elections. Voters only could choose between candidates of the Kuomintang and independent candidates. The two other legal parties apart from the KMT were not active parties, and their role was merely to enhance the legitimacy of the authoritarian rule of the KMT. Nonetheless, electoral competition in Town Councilmen elections, Town Chiefs elections, and County and City Councilmen elections was rather limited. Candidates who openly opposed the KMT were eliminated during the martial law period (1949-1987). The first new national elections, beginning in 1969, were conducted under the same rules; candidates who did not oppose the ruling party were the only form of political opposition. In 1975, for the first time, the opposition movement began to organize itself. The initially loose network of opposition leaders participated for the first time as an organized group in the 1977 county commissioner and city mayor elections. In the late 1970s and early 1980s, the opposition movement developed into a quasi-party, challenging the ruling party long before the fall of martial law.

With the establishment of the Democratic Progressive Party in 1986, Taiwan quickly turned into a full-fledged democracy, within only ten years, i.e. until the first Presidential elections in 1996. The first electoral victories of the DPP in 1989 and 1993 county commissioner and city mayor elections, deeply shocked the ruling KMT elite. In 1994, with the victory of Chen Shui-bian in the Taipei Mayoral elections – since Taipei is a stronghold of conservative political camp with a vast number of Mainland Chinese who or whose parents fled with Chiang Kai-shek from the mainland in 1949 – the Kuomintang was aware that it could lose any election, not just important local elections. Three years later in 1997, the KMT was, as it happens, surpassed by the DPP in absolute number of votes (i.e. island-wide, except Taipei and Kaohsiung); the KMT lost all important city and county magistrates losing a great amount of administrative power in the field of finance, policy administration, business and, of course, social affairs.

The KMT also faced fierce competition from within its own party. Three major parties split off from the ruling Kuomintang (the New Party in 1993, the People First Party in 2000 and the Taiwan Solidarity Union in 2001). In addition, in the 1990s, independent candidates and candidates of minor parties became another important force in the political landscape of Taiwan, winning a great number of seats in parliamentary elections. After 1994, elections in Taiwan were among the most fiercely contested in Asia (cf Copper, 1998). In South Korea, Hong Kong and Japan, democratic elections also became increasingly competitive in the last one and a half decades (see Table 1).

Table 1: Comparison of Political Factors Behind Welfare State Development in Taiwan, South Korea, Hong Kong and Japan

Factors	TAIWAN	SOUTH KOREA	HONG KONG	JAPAN
Democratic competition in elections and government formation	low (until 1986) medium (1986-1994) very high (after 1994)	none (until 1987) medium to high (after 1987)	none (until 1991) high (after 1991)	very low (until 1993) medium (after 1993)

Source: Christian Aspalter (2001a), 'Conservative Welfare State Systems in East Asia'.

In Chapter 2 of this book, the author first examines different approaches in welfare state theory and evaluates the current status quo. In order to promote a better understanding of the methods and the problematic of modern welfare state theory, he does not abstain from putting forward here a very critical account of recent theories, especially the regime theory of Esping-Andersen. In addition, a new definition of welfare state is put forward that does not refer to redistribution and government spending as core features of welfare state policy; and the term 'welfare state' is replaced with the more useful term 'welfare state system'.

Chapter 3 gives a basic understanding of the political context in Taiwan, introducing the political history of Taiwan beginning with the 16th century. The author also sketches the historical development of Republic of China in Mainland China until the end of the Civil War in 1949; and thereafter the history of the Republic of China on Taiwan. The study goes on to investigate the impact of Sun Yat-sen's Three Principles of the People on constitution and social policy. Thereafter, the author introduces the political system of Taiwan, beginning with the presidency; then, the five branches of government; and, finally, the five most important political parties (the Kuomintang, the Democratic Progressive Party, the New Party, the People First Party, and the Taiwan Solidarity Union).

In Chapter 4, the author goes on with a depiction of Taiwanese welfare state development. Giving a chronological account, the first part of this chapter focuses on the establishment and extension of social insurance systems, namely the Labor Insurance; then insurance schemes for military servicemen, employees and dependents of government organizations and private schools, Farmers' Health Insurance, National Health Insurance, and the Unemployment Benefit scheme of the Labor Insurance. In the second part of Chapter 4, the Taiwanese social assistance scheme is examined with special reference to the future challenge of providing social welfare for the rapidly augmenting elderly population. The author continues with a study of the growth of government expenditures in social welfare and the structural composition thereof. The last part of the chapter is formed by a retrospective of overall changes in Taiwanese welfare state policy. The Chapters 5 and 6 contain qualitative and quantitative studies of the 1997 and 1998 elections, which demonstrate the causal relationship of the degree of electoral competition in democratic elections and the number and extent of social welfare proposals of candidates and their parties.

The final chapter of the book concludes that it is not the factor economy that determines the course of welfare state development in Taiwan, as well as the rest of East Asian modern countries and most other developed regions of the world, but the factor democracy. The rising intensity of party competition in Taiwan after the formation of the Democratic Progress Party in 1986 and the New Party in 1993 is the major cause, besides the impact of a vast number of powerful social welfare movements, for the extension of the Taiwanese welfare state system.

In the 1990s, political parties that principally adopted an anti-welfare standpoint in social policy matters (that is, opposing an increase in contributory social insurance as well as non-contributory social assistance programs) began to support and even actively promote a series of comprehensive social insurance and welfare programs. Even in times of a troubled economy, due to intensified global economic competition and the Asian economic crisis of 1997, conservative governments vigorously continue to extend social security programs that increase both governmental welfare budgets and the cost of labor. Hence, there is no evidence of social dumping in the Tiger states. The opposite is true: that is to say, countries in East Asia construct welfare state systems, following somewhat the example of high developed welfare states in the West.

2 Welfare State Theory

There are many different ways how students of the welfare state may understand the phenomenon of welfare state development. Among the very different approaches, there are conventional and non-conventional ones. All of them, however, may be classified into three categories: First, we may observe the establishment and development of welfare states primarily from a national perspective and find explanatory theorems and theories describing the development in a certain country. Second, we may construct a theoretical model based on a group of countries, adding to the sum of national experiences the structural diversification and similarities among this group of countries. Third, there is the possibility of taking the world as a whole as the prime unit for the construction of welfare state theories.

The vast majority of welfare state theories are derived from a group of welfare states, and here again, almost exclusively that of Western Europe. Country studies may always contribute vital observations due to the possibility of in-depth analyses, such as descriptive historical studies, content analyses of election programs, and analyses of the process of a particular piece of legislation. Welfare state studies that include all parts of the world (cf Dixon, 1995, 1998) provide additional insights, but the trade-off between detail and general picture, by and large, exacerbates the difficulties of a researcher to select causal determinants from quasi-correlated variables (Aspalter, 2001b). Group studies are very exploitable, but the high number of new possibilities provided by this sort of analysis does not give rise to a large number of new conclusions.

The relative poverty of welfare state theory results from the complex relationships and the multidisciplinary methods that can – and have to – be applied in identifying the real causes behind certain developments, such as establishment, extension, reform, or retrenchment of welfare state institutions. Every social scientist knows about the risks that are involved in relating independent with dependent variables. Variable A, such as the share of the elderly population, and variable B, such as welfare state expenditures, may in fact seem to represent a causal relationship over short periods of time. But, over longer periods of time and in comparison with countries that apply different pension and health care systems, a correlation may easily lead to false conclusions, such as the share of the elderly in the population leads automatically to high welfare state expenditures. But, this is nonsense.

Welfare state expenditures depend in the first place from the kind of welfare state system applied. There are principally two kinds of social security systems, contributory and non-contributory ones. Contributory social security systems again may be partially or fully funded, which makes a vital difference in governmental welfare expenditures. Hence, simple correlations between variables do not lead to true conclusions every time. The famous poverty of theory in welfare state analyses, thus, is due to the rather unfortunate nature of a *not insignificant* number of studies on the welfare state.

Recently a major step forward in the evolution of welfare state theory have been brought about by Gøsta Esping-Andersen. Though it also caused a long-lasting flood of rather fruitful studies, his famous book, the Three Worlds of Welfare Capitalism (1990), also developed welfare state theory a great deal. However, there is still a series of fairly misleading conclusions. Would have been the methodology applied thoroughly and correctly in the 1990 book of Esping-Andersen, then there probably would have been no, or less, unlucky conclusions set forth by it.

The a bit confusing conclusions are: First, the impact of *liberal* social policy and *liberal* political parties, which designed the main column of the current Swedish social insurance system (introducing in the principle of universality) had been neglected. Esping-Andersen only ascribes Swedish welfare politics to the politics of the Swedish Social Democratic Labor Party, which indeed determined Swedish social policy exclusively, but only after 1960 (ibid., p. 27).

Second, Esping-Andersen confuses Christian democratic social policy in postwar Germany with that of archconservative Chancellor Otto von Bismarck at the end of the 19th century. He completely neglects new developments in German social policy after 1945, i.e. the coming of Christian democracy and with it a new era of pro-welfare social policies of two Christian parties (the CDU and the CSU), both of which have very strong labor union factions. However, Bismarck – on whose policies Esping-Andersen has focused, and from which he derived the findings in the first part of his 1990 book – pursued a strong anti-welfare stand and fought ferociously against the Christian labor movement and the large German Center Party (the first Christian democratic party in Germany), which both idealized the principles of Christian social teachings, i.e. the principle of solidarity and the principle of subsidiarity (Aspalter, 2001b).

Thirdly, Esping-Andersen does not distinguish between social policies and welfare systems of Japan, the United States, Australia and the United Kingdom. All these welfare state systems feature, from top to toe, different approaches to safeguard people's well-being. Japan, for a long time, promoted occupational welfare. The United States, avoided, to a large part, the establishment of social security systems (except in the field of pensions and unemployment), and strongly emphasizes tax exemptions. Social policy in Australia is based on highly targeted social policies, often combined with means tests. Conversely, the United Kingdom relied on universal, flat-rate social security system which represent exactly the type of social security systems applied in Sweden in the years before the 1960s.

Esping-Andersen applied the method of choosing a group of countries; however, he left out major regions of the world, and relied solely on selected quantitative data. Only limitedly, the 1990 study of Esping-Andersen let to truly new conclusion. The perspective applied – rather than the results presented by the study, which resemble sharply the findings of Richard Titmuss made in the late 1950s (cf Titmuss' 1958 book) – provide and lead the way to new insights for current and future generations of welfare state researchers.

We can profit greatly from his new theory of welfare state regimes, i.e. groups of welfare state systems that resemble each other (in other words, clusters of welfare systems). His new approach and his attempt to construct a new theory based on observations of more than one group of countries is of particular value, which enables a better understanding of welfare state development worldwide. The 1999 book *Social Foundations of Postindustrial Economies* simply tries to re-legitimize the propositions made in 1990. His reference to the existence of a *Homo Liberlismus*, a *Homo Familius*, and a *Homo Socialdemocraticus* – in other words, three groups of people that are fundamentally different – is a nice try but does not resemble much of a hardcore scientific study, i.e. being more journalistic in nature or at least semi-scientific.

But, we must not stop here. We need to go further and to find new ways of classifying welfare state systems in applying a consistent method of classification. Esping-Andersen applied three different parameters in classifying his three welfare state models: In the case of Sweden, he puts forward that the Swedish model is a social democratic model since the social democratic party was the dominant force behind welfare politics. In the case of Germany, he refers to historical determinants, such as the statist legacy of Germany. Again in the case of the United Kingdom and the United States, he argues with cultural determinants, i.e. especially the liberal work ethic of these countries (cf Esping-Andersen, 1990: 27f).

Every social scientist knows that one has to choose a criterion first and then classify the case studies, and not the other way around; and not to change the criterion with every case study (or group of countries). The second set of justification of his classifications, that is the degree of universalism, stratification and relationship between the state, the labor market and the individual, is much more convincing than the first one (cf ibid: 27f) and, thus, leaves sufficient room for new insights and theoretical advancement in other aspects.

In his 1990 book, he follows strictly the tripartite classification of Richard Titmuss (1958, 1974: 30-1, 1987: 262-3). His attempt to classify welfare state systems at large, however, was and still is the greatest success in recent welfare state theory, since before him virtually everyone focused solely on welfare state expenditures, and neglected different forms of social security provision.

Welfare state theorists ask not only, why governments across countries spend more or less money, how and why social security systems differ in one country from another? Moreover, they ask for the reasons why governments set up welfare state systems in the first place, why not earlier, why not later? Why do governments extend, change or retrench existing welfare state systems? Is ideology important? How important are culture and religion? Is poverty or unemployment the key to the understanding of the making of welfare states? And, how do various political and social determinants shape the course of welfare states systems?

Before we deal with the question why do welfare state systems emerge, extend and change?, we first need a definition of the 'welfare state', i.e. a welfare state system, itself. Since most social and political scientists think in terms of ideologies (which again differ from country to country), or are influenced via party membership, or personal believes, the term 'welfare state' is used differently by different groups of people, who not only have different political, but also different cultural backgrounds.

For purely conservative-oriented people, the welfare state is something negative, i.e. a system of high taxation and high redistribution from the more rich to the less rich, or from the majority to a poorer minority. For Christian democrats, i.e. moderate conservatives, who draw on Christian social thought of papal encyclicals and the teachings of influential pioneers of the Christian social movement (such as Bishop Ketteler), the welfare state is a means for achieving a greater societal well-being, which supports an occupationally divided societal structure (and, thus, avoids socialism and fascism), the institution of the family and the role of Christian churches with their strong welfare organizations (cf Aspalter, 2001b).

For representatives of the left political spectrum, the welfare state often is seen as the response of social democracy, socialism or communism to capitalism and its perceived, bad consequences for the lower and middle income segments of society. For most of them, a welfare state system connected with redistribution is a very positive thing, for which it is worth to bear the burden of high taxes.

But, the reality of welfare states – as Esping-Andersen started to show us – is manifold, and not twofold. Both Titmuss and Esping-Andersen, however, still believed in a basic dichotomy between the 'institutional' (i.e. full-fledged, high distributive) welfare state and the 'residual' (i.e. marginal, partly developed) type of welfare states. The variant of the continental European welfare state model, simply needed to be put into a third category, since it neither fit into the mold of the institutional, nor that of the residual welfare state.

The German model lacked both the 'liberal obsession with market efficiency and decommodification' (Esping-Andersen, 1990: 27; cf also Ferrera, 1993: 75). We cannot continue to think in a dichotomist way. There are many different forms of welfare states. It is for this reason why it is very useful to replace the term welfare state – which has a troubled history – with the term 'welfare state system' that implies in itself the existence of a variety of different forms of welfare states.

Welfare state systems may be defined simply as the sum of governmental regulations and provisions that aim at the enhancement of people's living conditions. Here we include, laws, regulations, and planning of all governmental institutions in the fields of employment, taxation, social insurance and social assistance, health care, education and housing. The government does not need to provide welfare services or benefits by itself; it may well support the private market, the family or non-governmental institutions in the provision of welfare. The concept of welfare state systems is easily understood by all sides, in all places; and it avoids the notion of a strong financial engagement of the state in provision of social welfare, as well as the notion of redistribution of financial resources from one segment of society to another.

The most interesting questions in welfare state theory are: Why do certain governments set up welfare state systems, why others not? And, why have governments of political parties of different political families decided for similar options in social policy? The answers are to be found in the study of political systems of these countries. The coexistence of divergence and convergence of welfare state systems worldwide can be explained by differences and similarities in the political arena of these countries.

The functionalist school of welfare state theory explains welfare state extension principally with an increase in the need for social welfare, such as industrialization, modernization, or the advance of capitalism. However, the extension of welfare needs is only a necessary, but not a sufficient condition for the establishment and the extension of welfare state systems. The conflict school of welfare state theory, however, provides a solution and overcomes the shortcomings of the functionalist tradition; i.e. the involvement of political parties and social movements in welfare politics.

In both the functionalist and the conflict tradition in welfare state theory, there are two streams of theories, the Marxist and the Non-Marxist stream. With regard to Marxist functionalist theories, theorists promote the idea that social policy is a response of capitalist nation-states that try to legitimize their unjust, capitalist rule with more or less generous welfare policies. The welfare state is understood as a logical development of capitalism to a stage where the state one the one hand must offer concessions to the oppressed majority; and to secure the capitalist mode of production, especially the accumulation of capital, on the other (Ramesh, 1984: 12). In this stream, a theory of legitimization crises of capitalism was put forward, which influenced a great deal of welfare state research from the 1970s onwards (cf e.g. O'Connor, 1973; Habermas, 1989).

Non-Marxist functionalist theories brought up the idea that the degree of industrialization of a certain country is the main cause for the amount of welfare state expenditures; economic growth as well as demographic and bureaucratic outcomes thereof, hence, were made responsible for the establishment and the extension of welfare state institutions (Wilensky and Lebeaux, 1958; Wilensky, 1975). Hence, the industrial society not only increases the need for vast social policy, but also the growth of massive bureaucratic organizations that provide the administrative power to engage in large-scale social security and redistribution programs. At the same time, the weakened ability of the family to take care of the elderly and children – due to the shrinking size of families and the increase of single-parent families – is adding to the growing welfare needs of an industrial or post-industrial society. Since non-Marxist functionalist theories identify industrialization as the main cause of welfare state development, they predict a common trend of convergence of welfare state systems, but fail to explain the persisting divergence of these systems.

Another representative of non-Marxist functionalist thought is the diffusion thesis (Collier and Messick, 1975). The diffusion thesis puts forward the idea that once social security programs are installed in one country, other countries successively copy these programs. The imitation of earlier social policies elsewhere would imply a sort of chain reaction responsible for welfare state formation and convergence around the globe. This thesis also fails to explain the deviant cases of welfare laggards, especially countries such as the United States and Switzerland.

In Marxist traditions of conflict theories, we find three major approaches:

1. the classical labor-centered approach, which follows the concept of the working-class mobilization thesis,
2. the new class/group-centered approach, which incorporates the important role of social groups and social classes,
3. the policy-centered approach, which recognizes the importance of ruling political parties, the logic of elections, and corporatism.

The classical labor-centered approach explains the different progress in the development of welfare states with the strength of left-wing parties and labor unions (cf e.g. Stephens, 1979; Korpi, 1980, 1983; Shalev, 1983a, 1983b; Esping-Andersen, 1985). However, this approach neglects to determine the role of other, non-leftist political parties and labor unions in welfare politics. The new class/group centered approach overcomes some difficulties of the classical working-class mobilization concept, i.e. it acknowledges the importance of farmers' and middle classes, besides the working class, and social groups that influence politics as well.

Claus Offe highlights the importance of social classes and social groups that penetrate politics via their market and organizational power (cf 1984a: 338-9, 1984b: 100-4). Other Marxist representatives of the conflict school also support the idea that the popular demands of social groups and classes in democratic regimes led to high government spending in the field of social policy (cf e.g. Marshall, 1964: 105f; Janoski, 1998: 149-54). Barrington Moore's class coalition thesis (1967) focuses on the importance of class coalitions between working, farmers' and middle classes in pushing the government to introduce and extend (distributive) welfare state policies.

The policy-centered approach advanced a greater inclusion of the policymaking processes in the development of welfare state theories. The policy-centered approach is not an exclusive Marxist approach, since there are also a great number of non-Marxist theorists who developed this approach side to side with the Marxists. The policy-centered approach analyses the impact of democratic participation (Rimlinger, 1971); electoral and party competition (Bartolini, 1995: 57-80; Downs, 1968; George, 1973: 14); election and party systems, strength and participation in government of *all* political parties (cf e.g. Wilensky, 1981; Castles, 1985b: 62-71; Baldwin, 1990); government coalition formation (cf e.g. Stephens, 1979: 101; Budge and Keman, 1990; Weir *et al.*, 1988: 16); distributional coalitions (M. Olson, 1976, 1982), and so forth. The studies of the policy-centered approach share a common focus on political determinants that shape social policy, especially political parties and democratic elections. The study on political parties and democratic elections constitutes the key to an understanding of the political and social forces behind welfare state development, and the political processes that are directly responsible for changes in welfare politics.

The Non-Marxist tradition of conflict theories developed also three major approaches:

1. the policy-centered approach, which recognizes the importance of ruling political parties, the logic of elections, and corporatism,
2. the state-centered/institutional approach, which concentrates on the impact of political systems and institutions on welfare politics, and
3. the elite-centered approach, which investigates the role of the governing elite in welfare politics.

The state-centered/institutional approach (cf Tocqueville, 1980: 61,71; Skocpol, 1987a, 1987b, 1992; Pierson, 1995) focuses on the nature of political systems (Rimlinger, 1971); power structures; governmental institutions; constitution-making; involvement in wars; national development formation processes; and types of political economies such as corporatist bargaining systems (Wilensky and Turner, 1987: 50-1).

The state-centered/institutional approach was mainly developed in the United States and helped a great deal in explaining the failure and the relative absence of social policies in America, compared to its European counterparts. The essential findings of this new approach are that differences in state structures matter, and that the lack of independent power of the state may also explain the lack and the failure of social policy programs. Furthermore, national mobilization for war efforts, national development formation processes, and strong governmental and corporatist institutions may also explain a large-scale extension of social policies. The elite-centered theories stress that a governing elite – i.e. those who hold positions of command in society – controls the mass of people (cf Bottomore, 1993: 25-6; M.E. Olson, 1970: 106-13).

What distinguishes this approach from the ones above is that it describes a particular group of e.g. governmental, economic and military elites that try to legitimate their power by means of welfare policies. It does not ascribe the power in social politics to social groups, social classes or political parties; but to governing elites. Max Weber led the development of the elite-power perspective and the related mass society perspective. Both elitist and mass society theories put forward explanations for the maintenance of the welfare state by a small minority, the governing elite. Weber noted that policy is always determined by a few people (cf Beetham, 1985: 106), mostly government officials and experts. Concerning the implementation of social welfare policies, Thoenes (1970: 177) notes that after political parties have accepted a series of basic ethical and socioeconomic principles 'all further government regulations on this matter can be regarded merely as rules, as technical details of a political programme which all have agreed upon'.

The study below is, of course, a single country study that focuses on the importance of democratization, and especially multi-party politics and party competition in democratic elections, for the development of welfare politics. Taiwan has experienced great changes in the last two decades of the 20th century, due to the coming of multi-party politics and democratization.

Before the fall of martial law in 1987, Taiwan was ruled by an highly authoritarian government. This regime only developed marginal social policies; most of insurance schemes and welfare benefits were directed toward privileged occupational groups that were vital for the maintenance of the authoritarian regime, i.e. military and civil servants, and teachers and staff of private schools. After 1987, the change from authoritarianism to democracy triggered a new wave of social policies, now addressing welfare needs of the needy and that of the mass of people. Democratic elections push competing political parties to advocate, by and large, the introduction of universal social policies, since they want to win elections with the support of a broad electoral basis.

The last part of this book consists of two in-depth analyses of the electoral process and its impact on social policies of major political parties, especially non-contributory social assistance schemes for the elderly. The correlation found is a causal correlation between increased party competition and the establishment of new, or extension of existing, welfare state programs. The qualitative in-depth analyses of this study avoid any quasi-correlation and prove its validity. Besides the thesis tested here that party competition is one of the major driving forces behind welfare state construction and development, there is another thesis that social welfare movements, and protest movements in general (especially the labor movement), also increase welfare state policies (cf Hsiao, 2001; S.Y. Ho, 1990; Aspalter, 2002).

3 The Political Context of the Welfare State in Taiwan

A Short History of Taiwan and the Republic of China

Taiwan

In the year 1517, Portuguese seamen who were sailing through the Taiwan Strait on their way to Japan sighted Taiwan. Astounded by the beauty of the island, they called it *Ilha Formosa*, meaning 'Beautiful Island'. The island was soon to attract many more strangers from far-away European lands. The Dutch first arrived in Penghu the main island of the Pescadores southeast of Taiwan in 1603. After the talks in Fujian, China assigned Taiwan to the Dutch as a trading post in 1623. In 1626, the Spanish sized control of the northern tip of Taiwan. In 1662, the Dutch lost control of Taiwan when general Koxinga fled there with his military, i.e. the remnants of the Ming dynasty. Cheng Ching, Koxinga's son, carried on the struggle of his father and imposed for the first time a Chinese style regime on the island.

In the 17th century, there were nine tribes of 'mountain aborigines', the Atayal; the Ami; the Bunun; the Paiwan; the Puyuma; the Rukaiand; the Saisiyat; the Tsou; and the Yami, all of which have survived. The Ami, Atayal, the Paiwan, and the Bunun are the four largest aborigine tribes today. Moreover, at that time, there were also eight tribes of flatland aborigines, the Babuza; the Hoanya; the Kavalan; the Ketagalan; the Luilang; the Pazeh Papora; the Siraya; and the Taokas. All Taiwanese aborigine tribes have completely different languages and cultures. They have migrated from far away places, such as Malaysia. To a certain extent, there even exists a relationship with the Maori people in New Zealand.

The flatland aborigines were completely assimilated by Chinese settlers through inter-marriage, and are now almost indistinguishable from the Chinese. Owing to the diversity of languages and the manifold divisions into racial groups, the aborigine tribes were not able to set up a common rule, and for that reason, have been pushed back by the masses of new Chinese immigrants (Ito, 2000). If it were not for the large share, i.e.

approximately two thirds, of Taiwan's land area that is occupied by high mountains that lack wider, accessible valleys, both the flatland and the mountain tribes would have become assimilated, and their cultures extinguished.

In 1683, the Ching Dynasty succeeded in incorporating China's last province not under its control, Taiwan. With the defeat of Cheng Ching, Taiwan came under Chinese rule. Between 1683 and 1850, Taiwan was part of Fujian Province and a seen as a remote island being barbarous, lawless and rebellious. Therefore, it was called the Wild East of China. There was a minor revolt against the governing regime every three years and a major one every five years. In 1887, Taiwan's status was upgraded to a full province of China. In 1984, for a short period after the Sino-Japanese War, a Republic of Democratic Taiwan had been proclaimed in Taiwan on, May 25, which only lasted 148 days (Ito, 2000; Long, 1991: 12-3). However, the Japanese took over the island after the Treaty of Shimonoseki the same year. For the next fifty years, Taiwan remained a colony of the Japanese empire.

The Cairo Declaration of 1943 assigned Chiang Kai-shek's nationalist China sovereignty over Taiwan. In 1945, Chiang Kai-shek sent general Chen Yi to Taiwan. At first the Taiwanese welcomed the nationalist Kuomintang regime as it replaced Japanese colonial rule. Soon, however, the Taiwanese felt that the Kuomintang was not a liberator, but just another colonial power. As a civil war broke out between Chiang Kai-shek's nationalist army and the communist People's Liberation Army of Mao Zedong, the Kuomintang practiced harsh political repression in Taiwan and excessively withdrew Taiwan's economic resources and transferred them to the mainland to support the war effort there.

In February 1947, Taiwan was at the brisk of revolution as on the evening of February 27, 1947, Monopoly Bureau agents beat a woman selling cigarettes on the black market in Tai Ping Street in Taipei and shot a protesting bystander. Large-scale protests followed, starting in Taipei and Keelung, and spreading out to Panchiao, Taoyuan and Taichung the next days, and then all over the island. This incident is known as the 2-2-8 Incident (referring to February 28). Though the government promised not to send in troops to suppress the protests, the Kuomintang sent more than 13,000 soldiers to Taiwan on May 8, 1947.

As the troops arrived at Keelung harbor, they indiscriminately shot into the houses and conducted ransom killings in order to crush the will of the people. The killings aimed not only to punish the people directly or indirectly involved in the incident, but also to eliminate the entire local intellectual and social elite who had received Japanese education; i.e. local politicians, teachers, professors, students, journalists, lawyers, artists and many more. The local elite regarded the culture and the administration of the newcomers from the mainland as being inferior to that of the Japanese. Taiwanese under Japanese rule exclusively spoke Japanese and were trained to become Japanese through and through. In the days and weeks following the 2-2-8 Incident, twenty eight thousand innocent people died (Ito, 2000; Gold, 1986; Lai *et al.*, 1991) as the result of the 'White Terror' of the KMT, which continued until the 1980s.

After the defeat in the civil war in 1949, hundred thousands (some researchers even suggest up to one and a half million) people streamed to Taiwan, mostly Kuomintang officials, soldiers and their families. The massive incoming of refugees from the mainland, in addition to the killings and the political suppression of the KMT, exacerbated the relationship between the Taiwanese (i.e. those who came to Taiwan during the time of the Ming and Ching Dynasties, speaking Minnan Chinese[1] and Hakka Chinese) and the Mainlanders (i.e. those who came to Taiwan between 1947 and 1949, speaking for the most part Mandarin Chinese). The political history in postwar Taiwan is, thus, determined by the rule of the nationalist Kuomintang dominated by Mainland Chinese over the long-term suppressed Taiwanese who – excluded from political participation – focused primarily on the acquisition of economic wealth. In the end, the new economic power of the Taiwanese also forced the ruling élites to incorporate them fully into the process of political decision-making.

The Republic of China

The Republic of China (ROC) was established in 1911 on the Chinese mainland by its founding father Dr. Sun Yat-sen. At that time, Taiwan and its surrounding islands were a Japanese colony. Sun Yat-sen yielded the presidency to Yuan Shih-kai, a military hardliner; only three months after Yuan became the first president of the Republic of China. In the succeeding years, Sun devoted himself to the task of educating the people, of making them understand the fundamentals of democracy and how they could uplift their economic standards. The first predecessor organization of the Kuomintang was the Hsing Chung Hui, the Revive China society, organized by Dr. Sun Yat-sen in 1894. The Tung Meng Hui, a organization that united all Revolutionists which had become the umbrella organization for Chinese anti-Monarchist forces at a conference in Tokyo, in 1905, was reorganized into the Nationalist Party, the Kuomintang, in 1911.

Between 1911 and 1924, the Republic of China was not fully established, regarding its governmental institutions, and regarding the territory under its control. These years were marked by numerous regional uprisings and revolutions. On March 12, 1925, when the unification of the country under the rule of the Kuomintang was apparently within reach, Sun Yat-sen died in Beijing (L.T. Chen, 1990; Moody, 1992: 16). The Kuomintang set up a government first in Southern China, in Guangzhou, in 1925. Chiang Kai-shek, a military strongman, then led the Nationalist forces on their victorious march from Canton toward the north in 1926.

Only in 1928, a unified nationalist government was set up in Nanjing. Thus, a nationalist government ruled the whole of China from 1928 until the outbreak of the second Sino-Japanese war in 1937. A provisional constitution and a draft constitution were promulgated on May 12, 1931 and May 5, 1936 (Zhao, 1996). In December 1946, while the civil war with the Communists was raging, the National Constituent Assembly was convened and a new Constitution promulgated on New Year's Day in 1947. In 1947 and 1948, in the area of China that was controlled by the Nationalists, elections were held for the National Assembly and the Legislative Yuan (the Second Chamber of the Parliament) with 2,961 and 760 representatives respectively (Copper, 1981a: 375).

On May 10, 1948, in the name of the ongoing civil war, the national government promulgated provisional amendments of the Constitution, i.e. the Temporary Provisions Effective During The Period of National Crisis[2] (TP, 1948). In Taiwan, these provisions were later known as the 'Temporary Provisions'. These provisional amendments enabled the President to enact martial law without the restriction of confirmation of the Legislative Yuan, as prescribed in Art. 39 and 43 of the Constitution (TP, 1948: Art. 1). Half a year later, on January 14, 1949, the President of the Republic of China, Chiang Kai-shek proclaimed martial law (ML, 1949).

In 1949, the Communist forces took over all of the mainland and the island province Hainan in the South China Sea. Taiwan, being located far away from the Chinese coast, on the contrary to Hainan, represented the last safe place of refuge for the Nationalist forces. Thus, by the end of 1949, the Kuomintang retreated to Taiwan and brought the whole of the Republic of China to Taiwan, including the Central Government with a vast number of parliamentary delegates, government official, soldiers, party officials and their family members. Hundreds of thousands, maybe more, people retreated within a short period of time to Taiwan. A small faction of the Nationalists went to Hong Kong, others to Japan or overseas.

The Republic of China on Taiwan

Having fled to Taiwan, the Nationalist forces faced two major problems, i.e. a possible attack from Mainland China and a revolution by the people of Taiwan. The loss of the civil war was based on two basic blunders of the Kuomintang, first the Kuomintang let the communist forces infiltrate the

Kuomintang during the time when both the Communists and the Nationalists fought against Japanese occupation of huge parts of Northeastern China, and second, the loss of the support of the masses.

Whereas the Communist movement, in its core, was a movement of poor farmers struggling for survival, the Nationalists relied on the support of the capitalists and the secret societies for financing their war efforts. In Taiwan, thus, the Kuomintang had to conduct a successful land reform[3] in order to guarantee the support of the masses of the people for the new regime and to prevent a Communist Revolution. Between 1949 and 1953, the Nationalist government put Sun Yat-sen's theory of the Three Principles of the People into practice; and in doing so it conducted a major land reform under the leadership of Chiang Kai-shek and Chen Cheng, the newly appointed Governor of Taiwan. The government first sold public land, reduced farm rents, and enforced the Land-to-the-Tiller Act that forced landlords to sell their land in return for commodity bonds and stocks of four major government enterprises (Fei *et al.*, 1979; S. Ho, 1978). Hence, the Nationalist government succeeded to conduct a comprehensive and very successful land reform, which laid the key fundaments for future economic development, prosperity and regime stability in Taiwan.

The geographic area now controlled by the Republic of China included Taiwan, the Pescadores situated in the southwest of Taiwan, and some tiny islands in the east of Taiwan; and two groups of small islands, Matsu and Kinmen islands, which are situated in front of the Chinese coast, and thus, very important for the defense of Taiwan. The islands of Matsu and Kinmen were part of the Fujian province in China before. Though, now being under control of the Taipei based Nationalist government, they are still regarded to belong to Fujian Province. In fact, the Republic of China on Taiwan tried, until the late 1990s, to represent all of China, however, it only controlled the territory of one full former province, i.e. Taiwan, and a tiny part of Fujian Province, i.e. the islands just mentioned.

In June 1950, the outbreak of the Korean War changed the stand of the Truman administration on American policy regarding the defense of Taiwan. The Taiwan Strait, being of high military importance as a main supply route for Korea and Japan, was then reckoned to be of high importance to American military engagements in East Asia. On June 27, President Truman ordered the Seventh Fleet to patrol the island against any military action by the Chinese Communists (Tien, 1992). Indeed, Taiwan faced an armed invasion of Communist forces twice, in 1954 and 1958 (Copper, 1981b).

In 1971, the Republic of China, though being a founding member, was expelled from the United Nations as it still claimed to represent the whole of China. The People's Republic of China (PRC) instead, from then on, represented the whole of China and occupied the seat in the Security Council of the United Nations formerly held by the ROC. The subsequent years, most of the nations in the Western World changed their diplomatic recognition from the nationalist ROC to the communist PRC. On December 15, 1978, the final blow to the international status of the ROC came with the announcement of the Carter Administration that the US was to establish formal diplomatic relations with the People's Republic of China while breaking up with the Republic of China. Taiwan was lucky in that the American public, the Senate, and the House of Representatives opposed the sudden abandoning of Taiwan. The Senate and the House passed the *Taiwan Relations Act* with an overwhelming majority, 85 to 4 in the Senate and 339 to 50 in the House of Representatives, in order to protect Taiwan's sovereignty, security, economic health, human rights, and forthcoming democracy in Taiwan (Copper, 1992).

In Taiwan, national elections had been 'frozen' for decades, as a result of a judicial decision of the Council of Grand Justices that was set up by the Judicial Yuan, the highest judicial organ of the State, according to Articles 78 and 79 (2) of the Constitution in order to interpret the Constitution with regard to the problem of holding national elections in a situation where most of the national territory is under control of Communist forces.

The National Assembly amended the Temporary Provisions in 1966 (TP, 1966; Art. 5) in order to give the President the power of calling for elections to fill vacancies in Central Government bodies, i.e. the National Assembly and the Legislative Yuan. Additional elections for the National Assembly and the Legislative Yuan were held beginning with 1969. The number of newly elected delegates that – on the contrary to those elected on the mainland – were to be reelected regularly, however, was only 15 and 8 respectively for the two chambers of the parliament in the first year. The numbers have risen gradually over the years (Wu, 1995). The first full election of the National Assembly and the Legislative Yuan in the Republic of China on Taiwan were in 1991 and 1992 respectively. In 1992, all senior cohorts that were elected on the mainland involuntarily retired as a result of another judicial decision of the Council of Grand Justices (Tien, 1996: 5).

During the 1970s and 1980s, the Kuomintang has been transformed from a Mainlander-dominated exclusionary authoritarian party to a pluralistic authoritarian party integrating more and more Taiwanese into policymaking (Tien, 1992: 10). Under martial law, civil and political rights have been largely restricted. Political parties other than the three established on the mainland were not allowed. These were the Kuomintang, and its two fraternal parties who did not actively recruit new members or win any election (Dickson, 1996), the China Youth Party and the China Democratic Socialist Party. The latter two were totally insignificant and served for a better cosmetic of the authoritarian political regime during the period of martial law.

The formation of new political parties had been illegal. Lei Chen and Fu Cheng, for example, had been sentenced to ten and more than 6 years respectively in jail for attempts to form the China Democratic Party in 1960 (Tien, 1996: 9; Huang, 2001b). Activists have been imprisoned, or they had been either killed directly or had to watch beloved family members being assassinated or maimed. The life stories of almost the entire leadership of the Democratic Progressive Party (the DPP), Taiwan's first opposition party, are full of political murders and attempted assassinations of their family members (including children, mothers and wives) and long-term imprisonment. To the numerous victims belong, for example, the mother and the twin daughters of former DPP chairman Lin Yi-hsiung who were assassinated on February 28,[4] 1980, by killers obviously hired by the KMT; and Wu Shu-jen, the wife of incumbent President, Chen Shui-bian. Wu Shu-jen was run over deliberately by a truck three times in an attempt to kill her in 1985 (Eyton, 2000).

Not less than 265 people have received the death penalty for reason of engaging in politics between 1949 and 1980. The entire elite of the DPP had been imprisoned for political reasons for many years, such as She Ming-teh, Lu Hsiu-lien Annette, Lin Yi-hsiung, Chen Chu and hundred others. Between 1949 and 1985, oppositional candidates had been imprisoned for a total number of 6,271 years and 11 months (Lu, 1997: 19).

Beginning with 1975, non-party independent candidates gradually formed the Dangwai (meaning 'outside the party'), the first organized political opposition in Taiwan (Wu, 1990: 91). Huang Hsin-chieh, a former legislator, was the head of the Dangwai movement. He first set up a Dangwai office in 1978 and chaired the first island-wide meeting of the Dangwai on December 5, the same year (Arrigo, 2000). It was a quasi-party that united anti-KMT forces. The 1977 elections for the Provincial Assembly and county magistrates saw the first spontaneous outburst of public anger since 1947. The Chungli Incident marked a new era of social discontent that ended in street protests.

By 1979, two major opposition groups have been formed. Both centered around their political magazines, *Formosa* and *The Eighties*. Their respective leaders, Huang Hsin-chieh and Kang Ning-hsiang, led these groups that, in the beginning, represented rather a grand coalition of individual oppositionists than a faction (Wu, 1995: 90-1). The first group that later became known as the Formosa faction was more radical and focused on mobilizing the masses by promoting democracy. The latter was more concerned with the problems of society and politics and tried to reform Taiwan's political system from within (Peng, 1986: 74-6). On December 10, 1979, the Human Rights Day a public speech of the opposition movement in Kaohsiung turned into street riots that left behind dozens of policemen injured. This event became to be known the Kaoshiung Incident. However, KMT forces carefully planned this incident (cf e.g. Schafferer, 2001: 91-2).

The Kaoshiung Incident constituted a major setback for the opposition movement, as almost the entire elite of the Formosa faction was tried in a military tribunal and received long-term prison sentences. This group was made up of Lu Hsiu-lien the leading women's activist who later become Vice-President of ROC in 2000; a number of future DPP chairmen, that were Yao Chia-wen, Huang Hsin-chieh, She Ming-teh, and Lin Yi-hsiung; future DPP secretary general Chang Chun-hong, as well as Chen Chu, a leading women's activist and two-time chairwomen of the Council of Labor Affairs, and Lin Hung-hsuan (Lu, 1997).

A second dominating faction emerged out of the Formosa faction, the New Tide faction. Tough, in the beginning, the distinction between these two factions were merely generational, the two quickly lived apart as the New Tide faction once again stuck to street action and tilted toward social democracy, while the mainstream Formosa faction represented a more moderate policy stand and promoted the idea of liberal democracy. Later on, the New Tide Faction promoted Taiwan Independence and forced the Formosa faction to support this goal and to add it to the charter of the Democratic Progressive Party at its Fifth Party Congress in October 1991 (Cheng and Hsu, 1996: 145; Arrigo, 1994; Soong, 1994: 78).

In the meanwhile, the KMT has undergone some vital changes. President Chiang Kai-shek died in 1975 and Vice-President Yen Chia-kan hold the presidency for the next three years. However, he was clearly only a figurehead of the State, as Chiang Ching-kuo, Chiang Kai-shek's son, already had become Prime Minister and Chairman of the Kuomintang. Chiang Ching-kuo also controlled the military and the security apparatus as he had already served as defense minister and head of the secret service. In May 1978, he was elected new president of the ROC (Copper, 1981b). Chiang Ching-kuo introduced a new period of reform of the Kuomintang, which had changed the major goals and tasks of the KMT, i.e. the abortion of the policy-focus to retake the mainland; the focus on solving firstly problems Taiwan was facing at the moment; a greater focus on elections, and the incorporation of the Taiwanese elite into the core of decision-making bodies within the State and the Kuomintang (Dickson, 1996).

Being pushed by fast expanding protests in the late 1970s and the first half of the 1980s, President Chiang Ching-kuo publicly declared in late

1985 – i.e. the year of the worst economic crises in the postwar history of Taiwan – that 'new policies must be established to address the issues derived from the changing tide and circumstances' (Tien, 1992: 9). At the KMT Central Committee Plenum in March 1986, Chiang Ching-kuo appointed an ad-hoc committee of high-ranking KMT officials to study and recommend concrete reform measures concerning the termination of both martial law and the ban of rival political parties; reform of the state structure; and reform of the KMT itself, such as a further incorporation of native Taiwanese into the rank and file of the KMT. After the imprisonment of several opposition activists among whom was the future President of ROC, Chen Shui-bian, in summer 1986, tens of thousand of people marched in the streets of Taipei to protest against the KMT (Chang, 1992).

On September 28, 1986, 132 members of the Dangwai movement established the first opposition party of the Republic of China since the KMT retreated to Taiwan. Still being illegal in Martial Law Taiwan, the DPP rallied for a big success in the first two-party elections in history of postwar Taiwan on December 6, 1986 with more than 25 percent of total votes captured by the DPP. On October 7, Chiang Ching-kuo announced that the end of martial law and the ban of opposition parties were soon to come. On October 15, he correspondingly pushed trough a resolution in a meeting of the KMT Central Standing Committee (Chang, 1992). Finally, the Emergency Degree, i.e. martial law, has been lifted on July 15, 1987.

The period from 1987 to the year 2000 was determined by the politics of reform of Lee Teng-hui. After Chiang Ching-kuo had passed away in January 1988, Lee Teng-hui took over as chairman of the KMT and President of the ROC. After being elected by the National Assembly for a new term as President in 1990, Lee Teng-hui announced in his inaugural speech on May 20 that he would put an end to the Temporary Provisions (see above). In fact, the Temporary Provisions had been terminated by May 31 the following year (Zhao, 1996: 149). With the constitutional amendment of April 1991, the presidential powers have been downgraded and the emergency decrees dissolved.

Though, in the beginning, many KMT heavyweights have thought of Lee Teng-hui as being a mere figurehead of the new government, Lee succeeded in gaining full control of the Kuomintang and in transforming Taiwan into a full-fledged democracy. The conservative elite of the KMT, i.e. those who were born at the mainland and fled to Taiwan with Chiang Kai-shek, opposed the numerous reforms of the President Lee Teng-hui, such as the indigenization of party power. Most of the party machinery – with the notable exception of the military and the veteran's organizations – had, for the most part, fallen into the hands of Taiwan-born party bureaucrats and politicians by 1994. This revolutionary development was quickly successful at county and provincial levels and, then, also at central government level and the central committee of the party (Tien, 1996: 12; cf Clark, 1989: 132).

As members of the old guard of the KMT were too upset for loosing their dominant position within the party, they formed the New KMT Front that served as the mainstay of the non-mainstream faction inside the KMT on February 9, 1990. At first, Lee Teng-hui handled fierce opposition within his party with the nomination of Hau Pei-tsun (Hao Bo-tse) – a Mainlander, a military strongman, and leader of the non-mainstream faction – as Prime Minister in May 1990 (Huang, 1996). The split between the mainstream and the non-mainstream faction of the KMT resulted in the formation of the New Party in summer 1993. From 1994 to the year 2000, the KMT hegemony had been reinstalled under the leadership of President and Party Chairman, Lee Teng-hui. The constitutional amendment of 1994, introduced direct elections of the President. In March 1996, Lee Teng-hui has been elected President with 54 percent of votes.

The DPP won considerable support not only in national elections, but also, and even more, in local elections. The relative sluggishness of DPP electoral results on national level is to be traced back to the precarious political situation of Taiwan in the late 1980s and the 1990s. This was especially the case in the 1991 National Assembly Election and the 1996 Presidential Election where the proclamation of Taiwan Independence as the goal of the DPP and the threat of Mainland China that was holding military exercises in front of the shores of Taiwan respectively resulted in bad election results for the DPP. On local level, the DPP celebrated big triumphs since the end of the 1980s. In 1989, the DPP candidate You Ching became County Commissioner in Taiwan's largest constituency, Taipei County. In 1994, the year of the elections for the Governor of Taiwan Province and the mayors of Taipei and Kaohsiung, Chen Shui-bian won the Taipei mayoral election, and thus, was the first opposition leader to become mayor in Taiwan's capital city.

In the 1998 mayoral elections, the DPP lost the Taipei mayoral election to Ma Ying-jiou, the popular candidate of the KMT, who being a Mainlander could attract the votes of the large Mainlander electorate of the New Party in Taipei. In Taiwan's second largest city, Kaohsiung, however, the KMT candidate Wu Den-yih also lost, to surprise of even the greatest positivists inside the DPP, to Frank Hsieh (Hsieh Chang-ting) of the DPP. In the 1997 county commissioner and city mayor elections, the DPP won, for the first time, more votes in island-wide[5] election than the ruling KMT. The KMT won in eight counties (out of 23 counties and cities!), which are relatively the most backward, least developed and most remote ones.[6]

With the 1997 county commissioner and city mayor elections the KMT lost most of its power bases all over Taiwan and the victory of the DPP in national elections was merely a matter of time. The 1998 Legislative Yuan elections did, however, not yet mean a changeover of power, but rather a contemporary consolidation of KMT power in the Legislative Yuan.

After the defeat of Chen Shui-bian in the Taipei Mayoral race of 1998, Chen was free for the nomination as the DPP candidate in the 2000 Presidential elections, which he astoundingly won. Lee Teng-hui's designated successor, former Prime Minister Lien Chan, was defeated by former Taipei Mayor Chen Shui-bian, and also by independent candidate James Soong (Song Chu-yu) in the 2000 presidential election. Chen Shui-bian became the tenth President of the Republic of China and the first President of the Republic of China who was not a member of the Kuomintang. The long-term ruling KMT not only lost the presidency in this elections, but also the majority in the Legislative Yuan owing to the formation of a new party, i.e. the People First Party that was formed by former KMT party heavyweight James Soong. Soong announced the formation of a new party just one day after the elections, which was called the New Taiwanese People's Party, and renamed two days later into the People First Party.

The Three Principles of the People and the Constitution of the ROC

The Three Principles of the People

In the preamble of the ROC Constitution it is stated that the National Constituent Assembly of the Republic of China adopts the Constitution 'by virtue of the mandate received from the whole body of citizens, in accordance with the teachings bequeathed by Dr. Sun Yat-sen in founding the Republic China, and in order to consolidate the authority of the State, safeguard the rights of the people, ensure social tranquility, and promote the welfare of the people'. The threefold emphasis of the consolidation of state authority, people's rights and social tranquility and the welfare of the people refer to the 'The Three Principles of the People' (San Min Chu I) of Sun Yat-sen.

Witnessing the defeat of China in the Sino-Japanese War (1894-1895) and bearing in mind all the defeats China suffered at the hands of other countries in the last couple of centuries, Dr. Sun Yat-sen, a trained medical doctor, set up a theory that ought to protect the people of China and, hence, the country of China. The theory put forward by Sun Yat-sen was summarized in his 'Three Principles of the People'. These were the principle of nationalism (i.e. national unity), the principle of democracy, and the principle of livelihood (i.e. the well-being of the people). In 1895, after a hasty attempt of revolt that failed, Sun Yat-sen went to Japan, America and Europe. By studying the history as well as the social and political institutions of these countries he worked out his three basic principles that were to safeguard a better future for China (Sun, 1990).

The first one, nationalism, addressed the need of China to build a state. Traditionally, Chinese society only emphasized family and clan groups. Solidarity across family and clan borders, by and large, was unknown to Chinese up to the 20th century. As a consequence of that China has become 'the poorest and weakest state in the world, occupying the lowing position in international affairs'. Therefore, the Chinese people 'must espouse Nationalism and employ the national spirit to save the country' (ibid.: 5). Sun Yat-sen criticized the comfort of many Chinese who comforted themselves with the fact that China was only a semi-colony, and not a full colony. He pointed out that China in reality is 'being crushed by the economic strength of the Powers to a greater degree than if it were a full colony' (ibid.: 10). Furthermore, Sun Yat-sen referred to the Jewish and the Polish people who for many centuries did not have a state of their own. Having studied in Hong Kong under British rule, Sun Yat-sen saw the danger that China would be subjugated and destroyed by England or America (ibid.: 15,17). In the eyes of Sun Yat-sen, the aim of nationalism was to guarantee the survival of China, its people and culture; and to guarantee economic and social well-being of the Chinese people.

The second principle, i.e. democracy, was no less important than the first one. Sun Yat-sen clearly stressed that if China wanted to be strong and the revolution to be effective, China must espouse the cause of democracy. He observed the world tendency of a growing number of democracies that put an end to autocratic regimes (ibid.: 63). In addition, Sun Yat-sen emphasized the long-term plague of Chinese history, i.e. an ongoing succession of wars for the throne of the country. Wars in China were always wars of one king with the other, of one ruler with the other, and not wars over religion or wars over freedom. Thus, democracy would prevent, to a great deal, the probability of civil wars in China as it would replace the struggle for power formerly conducted by military means by a struggle for power conducted by democratic means (ibid.: 65).

Regarding the form of governmental institutions, Sun Yat-sen highlighted the importance of the Federal Constitution of the United States that was the first written constitution that separated the three branches of government in securing the advance of democracy. Thus, the United States was the wealthiest and most powerful nation in the world. Far from simply copying the Federal Constitution of the United States, Sun Yat-sen took the tripartite model of government and improved it by adding two additional branches of government that guarantee the proper conduct of government employees, the ministers, the prime minister and even the president.[7] Thus, the model of government proposed by Sun Yat-sen added to the tripartite model of government a system of 'compact and effective control' of the government (ibid.: 141).

The third principle put forward by Sun Yat-sen was the principle of livelihood (Min Sheng Chu I). While the first two principles are also responsible for preconditions of people's livelihood, the third principle goes into more detail and provides an action plan for social and economic policies. Sun Yat-sen realized that social problems, and not material forces (as proposed by Marxism), are the main determinant of the course of History. He identified subsistence as being at the heart of social problems. The principle of livelihood addresses the problem of subsistence (ibid.: 155). Sun Yat-sen proposed major policies for social and economic reform that have been successfully applied earlier by Germany, Great Britain and the United States which are: nationalization of transportation and communication, direct taxation or the income tax, and socialized distribution or co-operative societies (ibid.: 158, 171).

A major point made by Sun Yat-sen, was the importance of an equal distribution of land. Equalization of land ownership should be reached by a combined tax and land purchase system by which the land owners can assess the value of their land by themselves and taxes will be collected according to this given land value; the government, in addition, has the right to purchase the land at the price that the landowners told the government it would be worth. Thus tax evasion would be avoided and the real value of land would be offered by the government for any land purchases. From then on, *all increase* in land value shall revert to the community.[8] This is because the increase in land value, so Sun Yat-sen, is due to 'improvements made by society and to the progress of industry and commerce' (ibid.: 178).

Moreover, Sun Yat-sen stressed the need to build extensively means of communication, railroads and waterways, and to develop primary industries, such as mining and agriculture. The economic policies given are quite precise, such as in the case of the agricultural industry. Agricultural production, so Sun Yat-sen, ought to be expanded by the 'use of machinery, use of fertilizers, rotation of crops, eradication of pests, manufacturing of agricultural products, building waterways and railroads for the transportation agricultural products, and prevention of natural disasters' (ibid.: 188). Finally, Sun Yat-sen stresses the importance of the clothing industry for the well-being of the people. The State 'should establish clothing factories everywhere on a large scale' and the factories 'should manufacture the clothing needed by the people' and everyone 'should be supplied with the necessary clothing; not one person should be left out'. Lazy vagabonds and loafers should be 'converted into honorable laborers'. Sun Yat-sen concludes that when all people 'have a share in production, then there will be enough to eat and to wear, homes will be comfortable, and the people will be content, and the problem of livelihood will be solved' (ibid.: 212).

The Influence of the Three Principles on the Constitution

Sun Yat-sen's theory of Three Principles of People has influenced greatly the content of the ROC Constitution. Regarding the content, we note that all personal and political rights and democratic institutions of a modern democracy have been laid down in the Constitution of the ROC in the year 1947. Article 9 provides that except those in active military service, no person shall be liable to court-martial. Articles 11 to 13 guarantee the freedom of speech, teaching, writing, and publication; the freedom of privacy of correspondence; the freedom of religious belief, respectively. The freedom of assembly and association; the right to present petitions, lodge complaints, and institute legal proceedings; and the rights of election, recall, initiative and referendum are granted by Articles 14, 16 and 17 of the Constitution.

With regard to elections, the Constitution of 1947 demanded the elections of the National Assembly (C, Art. 26) that in return elect the president and the vice-president by the National Assembly (C, Art. 27), and the election of Legislative Yuan, the Lower House of the Parliament (C, Art. 64) and the election of the Control Yuan (C, Art. 91) by Provincial and Municipal Councils. In Article 124, the Constitution demands the election of County Councils. The National Assembly, the Legislative Yuan and County Councils – under normal conditions – were to be elected by the citizen of the Republic of China. Articles 129 to 136 regulate elections of these governmental bodies. However, from the declaration of martial law in 1949 until the lift of martial law in 1987, the constitutional right of personal and political freedom was suspended. During the period of martial law the Taiwan Garrison Command, a military organization responsible for internal security, could try anyone that it accused of committing a political crime in military courts (Glough, 1981: 351).

According the principle of livelihood, the ROC Constitution clearly promotes the establishment of a welfare state in Taiwan. Article 155 of the ROC Constitution provides that the State 'shall establish a system of social insurance to promote social welfare. To the aged and the physically disabled who are unable to make a living, and to victims of extraordinary calamities, the State shall provide appropriate assistance and relief.' In addition to that, Article 157 lays down that the State 'in order to improve national health, shall establish extensive services for sanitation and health protection and a system of public medical care'.

In a 1992 special session, the National Assembly drafted Additional Article 18 (3) of the ROC Constitution, which stipulates that the State 'shall implement health insurance and promote the research and development of modern and traditional medicine'.[9] The State, furthermore, 'shall protect motherhood and carry out a policy for the promotion of the welfare of women and children' (C, Art. 156). In Articles 153, the Constitution safeguards the protection of laborers and farmers, as well as woman and children doing manual labor. Article 154 emphasizes the importance of harmony and cooperation between labor and the management and demands that conciliation and arbitration of labor disputes shall be prescribed by law. The State's duty to provide proper employment opportunities to those who have the ability to work was laid down in Article 152. Furthermore, the State 'shall widely establish financial institutions for the common people so as to relieve unemployment' (C, Art. 150).

The fifth section of the Constitution (C, Articles 158 to 167), in addition, focuses on the State's duty to promote education and culture in context of national building. Article 159, for example, stipulates that all citizens 'shall have an equal opportunity to receive education'. As a consequence thereof, the government extensively invested in the public school system, including a wide-ranging network of government colleges and universities. The Constitution demands that the various levels of government spend a certain share of their budgets for education, science and culture. Article 164 states that funds earmarked for education, science, and culture shall be, in respect of the Central Government, not less than 15 percent of the total national budget; in respect of the Provincial Government, not less than 25 percent of the total Provincial budget; and in respect of the Municipal or County Government, not less than 35 percent of the total Municipal or County budget.

Article 142 demands that the national economy 'shall be based on the Principle of People's Livelihood and shall seek to effect the equalization of land rights and regulation of private capital in order to assure an equitable distribution of wealth and sufficiency for the people's livelihood'. 'Privately owned land shall pay taxes according to its value and may be purchased by the Government according to its value ... The State shall levy a land value increment tax on any land whose value has increased not through the application of labor or capital, and the proceeds therefrom shall be used for the people at large' (C, Art. 143).

Furthermore, Article 144 stipulates that in principle public utilities and enterprises of a monopolistic nature 'shall be under public operation'. In cases permitted by the law, however, they may be operated by private citizens. Article 145 (2) guarantees the encouragement and assistance from the State for cooperative enterprises. Article 146 addresses the need of applying scientific techniques to agriculture; developing water conservancy; increasing the productivity of land; improving agricultural conditions; developing agricultural resources; and fostering the industrialization of agriculture.

Finally, we may note that the policy guidelines given by the Three Principles of the People of Sun Yat-sen and the provisions of the Constitution of the ROC that was built these principles, indeed influenced the policies of the State in Taiwan a great deal. Striking examples for this are: the effective land reform, nationalization policy of main enterprises, the heavy focus on industrial policy and equal distribution of wealth, the conduct of local elections with the acceptance of independent candidates even during the whole time of martial law, the peaceful transition to democracy in the 1980s, and the early implementation of a social security systems in the 1950s.

The Presidency

In the history of the Republic of China, the form of government changed a couple of times. In the beginning, a cabinet system had been installed between 1925 and 1928, and reinstalled between 1931 and 1936. In the meantime, and again after 1936, the presidential system of government had been put in place. During the time when a cabinet system was installed, the president was merely a figurehead of the State who was not allowed to hold any other government, party and military position at the same time. The real power of the State lay in the hands of the National Government Council. However, under the presidential system, besides being the head of the State, the president also held the post of the chief executive of the government, chairperson of the Nationalist Party, the Kuomintang, and the commander in chief of the nationalist army.

Under the 1947 Constitution, there can be either a presidential or a cabinet system (Zhao, 1996). When the president simultaneously also holds the leading posts of the party and the military then the government system clearly is a presidential one where all the powers of the State were united, and exercised by the president alone. For the most part of the postwar Republic of China, this had been the case. The president, according to Article 36 of the Constitution, had the supreme command of the army, the navy and air force. The president also appointed the President and Vice-President of the Executive Yuan, and the Ministers (C, Art. 55, 56).

Nonetheless the ROC Constitution, as of 1947, also implemented a check of powers between governmental institutions. Until the constitutional amendment of 1994, the President and the Vice-President of the Republic of China was to be elected and recalled by the National Assembly (C, Art. 27). Thus, the powers of the President were granted by the National Assembly that was to be elected by the people in (all parts[10] of!) the ROC, and exercised the 'political rights on behalf of all the citizens of the country' (C, Art. 25). In addition, the Prime Minister and the Ministers of the State are responsible to the Legislative Yuan who may intervene in policymaking and confirm the appointment of the President of the Executive Yuan by the President of the Republic of China (C, Art. 57, 55). Thus, it is vital to the power of the President that he or she also is the chairperson of the ruling party. It may happen that the President may not be the chairperson of his party (if he or she has joined a party at all), or that the Legislative Yuan is dominated by another party or other parties. Then, the powers of the State reside largely in the hands of the Executive Yuan (the Cabinet) once it has the full backing of a majority in the Legislative Yuan.

The Five Branches of Government

Most Western countries only have a tripartite structure of government. The Constitution of the Republic of China, however, demands a quintuple structure for the Central Government. The five branches of government are the Legislative Yuan, the Executive Yuan, the Judicial Yuan, the Examination Yuan and the Control Yuan. The Legislative Yuan is the highest legislative organ of the State and is composed of members elected by the people. Until the constitutional amendment of 1999, the members of the Legislative Yuan were elected for a term of three years on the basis of both geographical and occupational representation (C, Art. 62, 64, 65).

The Executive Yuan, i.e. the Cabinet, is the highest administrative organ of the State. The Executive Yuan consists of a president, a vice-president, a prime minister, a number of ministers, chairpersons of commissions, and ministers without portfolio (C, Art. 54). The Judicial Yuan is the highest judicial organ of the State and responsible for the trial of civil, criminal, and administrative cases and the disciplinary punishment of public employees. Moreover, it has the power to interpret the Constitution and to unify the interpretations of laws and ordinances. The President of the Republic appoints, upon confirmation of the Control Yuan, the President and the Vice-President of the Judicial Yuan and a number of Grand Justices (C, Art. 77-9).

The establishment of the Examination Yuan and the Control Yuan had been promoted by Sun Yat-sen in order to prevent corruption and to guarantee a more equal distribution of powers. Until the constitutional reform in 1997, it was up to the Control Yuan to impeach the President of the ROC; thereafter the Legislative Yuan gained the power of impeaching the president. The presidents and the members of the Examination Yuan are, upon confirmation of the Control Yuan, appointed by the President of the ROC (C, Art. 84). They conduct the examination and evaluation of government employees. The Control Yuan exercises the powers of consent, impeachment, censure and auditing (C, Art. 90) and its members are elected by Provincial and Municipal Councils, the Local Councils of Mongolia and Tibet, and Chinese citizens residing abroad, so the Constitution (Art. 91).

The Parties

The China Nationalist Party

History and Development The China Nationalist Party, which is widely known as the Kuomintang, has been established in 1911 by Dr. Sun Yat-sen, the founding father of the Republic of China. First, it carried the name of Nationalist Party[11] (the 'Guo Min Dang'). After having shortly changed its name into China Revolutionary Party (the 'Chung Hua Ge Ming Dang') from 1916 to 1919, the party finally adopted the name of China Nationalist Party (the 'Chung Guo Guo Min Dang') in 1919.

Dr. Sun Yat-sen, set up the main ideology of the party, which had been of far-reaching consequences to the political, societal, and economic development of the Republic of China, but this only after its retreat to Taiwan. This is mainly explained by two factors: first, the fact that the 1947 Constitution of the Republic of China, which was of high importance to the political development of Taiwan in the second half of the 20th century, clearly contains the major teachings of Dr. Sun Yat-sen, especially the Three Principles of the People; and second, the fact that the Three Principles of People were a compulsory subject at all medium and higher levels of educational institutions in Taiwan. These principles were the principle of nationalism, the principle of democracy and the principle of people's livelihood. They were understood, subsequently, by all citizens and also highly respected by all policy-makers within the KMT.

The developmental history of the KMT mirrored the history of China, and then, after the loss of the Civil War, the history of Taiwan. The fight against the last Chinese Empire (1895-1911); the fight against local military chiefs (1911-1928); the fight against the Japanese (1937-1945); the fight against Mao Ze-dong's Communist forces (1945-1949); the fight against local elites and the independence movement in Taiwan (1947-1986); the fight for economic development (1949 to the present); the fight against diplomatic isolation (1971-2000); and the fight against offspring factions and parties of the KMT (1989 to the present). With regard to the KMT during its rule over Taiwan, we note that the KMT has transformed itself from an authoritarian regime, which notoriously disregarded and fought against the will and the needs of the people, into a democratic regime that abandoned its radical, authoritarian elements in order to address the wants of the people rather than that of party cadres and local elites. The history of the KMT, demonstrates its struggle for survival under ever-changing domestic and international circumstances. How did the KMT manage to survive and to cope with major problems and, most of all, to preserve the political hegemony under its reign for such a long time?

First, there is the long-term perspective in policy developments, i.e. its perseverance in getting things done. The Three Principles of the People having been developed in the first two decades of the 20th century, for example, were no earlier implemented as in the years following 1949, after the retreat of the KMT to Taiwan; but, then they were implemented one at a time over the following decades, i.e. the design of the constitution; land reform; social insurance; adherence to one-China policy (the importance of which began to fade in the 1990s); introduction of democracy and that of a wide range of welfare state institutions.

Second, the KMT learned a crucial lesson from the defeat by the Communists on the mainland who watched and addressed – on the contrary to the KMT – the needs of the common people from the very beginning. The rapid completion of land reform and the introduction of labor insurance program were direct consequences of the defeat on the mainland.

Third, there were several major structural reforms of the State via constitutional[12] and governmental reforms;[13] and the party itself via new electoral systems of the Central Committee and the Central Standing Committee, as well as new candidate nomination systems and the incorporation of Taiwanese in policymaking (Huang, 1996: 115-25; Dickson, 1996: 53). In 1972, the reform of the central party organs included new organs, new personnel, and a partial reassignment of responsibilities, especially for the most vital departments for the future of the KMT, i.e. those that dealt with elections, the popular support of the party, personnel appointments, the implementation of party policies, and the recruitment of new members (Dickson, 1996: 50).

Fourth, the KMT began to incorporate a *brainy* elite into chief party posts, who came to determine overall policymaking by the mid-1990s. From the early 1970s to the early 1980s, the majority of Central Standing Committee members have academic degrees, especially in social sciences and humanities, but also in natural sciences and engineering (Dickson, 1996: 51).

Fifth, the KMT applied a permanent mix between cruel political measures and friendly policies[14] during the time of martial law, which was followed by an era of enormous pragmatism.[15]

The internal reforms of the KMT in the second half of the 20th century deserve further discussion. The two most important party organs beside the chairperson of the party are the Central Committee and the Central Standing Committee. The delegates of the National Congress elect the members of the Central Committee and the Central Standing Committee. However, from 1952 to 1988 all candidates have been nominated by the chairperson who, thus, gained extensive control over the party at that time. The National Congress only elected the Central Committee members by block vote. In 1988, the majority of delegates of the National Congress was, for the first time, democratically elected. Furthermore, since 1988 the delegates may also nominate a list of candidates for all seats of the Central Committee, and since 1993, the block voting system had been replaced by the limited vote system in which the delegates exercised more influence on election outcomes.

The Central Standing Committee was the most powerful decision-making body of the party. Until 1993, all candidates were elected by the party leader and passed unanimously. Thereafter, all candidates for half the seats plus one were still nominated by the party leader, and the remainder were provided by both the party leader and the joint signature of the delegates (Jiang and Wu, 1992: 80; Huang, 1996: 122-3).

An important feature of party politics and the electoral performance of the party is the candidate nomination procedure. In the first years after having arrived in Taiwan, the Kuomintang had not yet developed its grassroots organizations. Thus, in choosing its candidates for the local elections the KMT applied a strategy of selective support of both KMT and independent candidates of whom KMT thought would guarantee its future control of local politics. In the 1954 and 1957 Provincial Assembly elections, the KMT held primaries, but the results of these primaries were not publicized which constituted a major control element of the ruling elite. Since 1957, the KMT conducted opinion inquiries of members, and since 1980, an evaluation of its cadres. However, these measures were introduced without invoking any obligation of party leaders. Between 1989 and 1992, at the time of major dispute between the KMT mainstream and non-mainstream factions, a system of closed primaries was applied. Whereas the primary results served as a major basis for nomination in 1989, it was so to a lesser degree – but still important – in the nomination procedures for the 1991 and 1992 elections (Huang, 1996: 124-5).

The membership structure of the KMT has been changing over the years from being heavily male dominated and Mainlander dominated, to a less male dominated and heavily Taiwanese dominated one. In 1976, 82.9 percent of KMT members had been males (Dickson, 1996: 37). Due to the hefty explosion of overall membership numbers, from 950,993 in 1969 to 2,617,651 in 1992, the percentage of male members had been fallen slightly since 1969. The percentage of Mainlanders in overall membership has dropped from 60.6 to 30.81 percent over the same period of time. The percentage of Taiwanese members accordingly rose from 39.4 to 69.19 percent (Dickson, 1996: 37; Huang, 1996: 115). The occupational structure of the KMT has also changed significantly in the past. In 1952, 39.6 percent of party members were soldiers. This share declined to 5.8 percent by the year 1974. The share of party and government officials and educators, however, rose continuously from 18.6 percent in 1952 to 24.5 percent in 1986. The shares of farmers, workers, entrepreneurs, students, and the new middle classes also rose significantly in the past decades (Dickson, 1996: 59).

The composition of Central Committee members also experienced a hefty reverse of the power balance between Mainlanders and Taiwanese. Whereas Taiwan-born members only counted for 3.1 percent of total Central Committee members in 1952, they built up the majority of members in 1993 with 53.3 percent of total membership. As to the powerful Central Standing Committee, we note that until 1957 all members were born at the mainland. The first Taiwan-born member joined in that year. By 1993, 20 out of 35 members of the Central Standing Committee (i.e. including four party vice-chairmen) were Taiwanese, which adds up to 57.1 percent of members. In 1993, only three members of the Central Standing Committee belong to the military elite (Huang, 1996: 118-20).

Factions and Policies In Taiwan politics, there are two major types of political factions, local factions and central party factions. Local factions are bound to the county and city level. The activity of a local faction usually is bound to the borders of one single constituency. Central party factions usually split the party at the central party level. Local factions, on the contrary to central party factions, are not characterized by different ideologies and policy stands. In the 1990s, there were more than one hundred local factions in Taiwan (Huang, 1996: 127). The numerous local factions were created by an attempt of the KMT to check the balance of power of town chiefs, and thereby, to maximize that of the central party. Local factions, in addition, were used to help the KMT to win local elections (Bosco, 1994: 136, 138). The history of local factions in Taiwan, thus, begins with the first local elections hold in 1950. In that year, there were Town Councilmen elections, Town Chiefs elections, and County and City Councilmen elections. Local factions provided the core of support in all elections.

As first national elections were delayed until 1969, the culture of local faction politics was tied to the boundaries of their respective constituencies. Local factions could not be penetrated by the KMT as they were built exclusively on informal ties. The core leaders of these factions determined who was included and who was excluded from the faction. Local factions were hold together by social ties among kinship, between patrons and their clients, friends, classmates, etc. A family that loyally supports a faction's candidates can rely on the faction leader for help, such as the distribution of jobs in the local government and elsewhere; infrastructural improvements, such as roads, traffic lights, community centers, etc.; bureaucratic problems of businesses, such as licenses, tax audits, pollution standards, land-use regulations, electric power, etc.; favorable loans and credits from state-owned commercial banks; special zonings for public construction projects and urban planning; local government public contracts; special permits for banking, bus companies, credit unions, etc.; and the numerous problems of ordinary citizens (Bosco, 1994: 119, 125; Tien, 1996: 19).

If we look at the wide range of benefits, on the one hand, available to voters that support a winning faction and, on the other hand, the benefits available to those elected who, then, can profit from their wide-ranging patronage system, we can grasp the importance of these local factions in policymaking. In recent years, more and more faction leaders that were not nominated by the KMT either run as independent candidates or supported candidates of the opposition party, the DPP. Since the introduction of national elections, the existence of local factions also spurred the emergence of central party factions and parties that tried to profit from factional cleavages in local politics.

The liberalization and democratization of intra-party politics led to the emergence of 18 central KMT party factions between April 1988 and September 1993 in the Legislative Yuan alone. However, these factions were again divided into two major factions, the mainstream faction supporting President Lee Teng-hui and the non-mainstream faction supporting Hau Pei-tsun. The former, under the leadership of the Collective Wisdom Club in the Legislative Yuan, was established on April 22, 1988;

and the latter, under the leadership of the New KMT Alliance, on February 9, 1990 (Huang, 1996: 126-9). Hau Pei-tsun became Prime Minister in May, 1990, following a major dispute between the Mainlander elite inside the KMT and President Lee-Teng-hui about the nomination of Lee Yuan-tsu as candidate for Vice-President in the 1990 Presidential election (Chu and Lin, 1996: 84).

The mainstream and non-mainstream factions did not have local offices, on the contrary to their local pendants, and their ideological and policy cleavages were fundamentally different. The non-mainstream faction favored broader economic and cultural exchange with Mainland China while Lee Teng-hui resisted the pressure to lift the ban on direct air and sea links with the mainland. The non-mainstream faction, furthermore, considered Taiwan independence activists secessionists and urged the government to continue taking legal actions against the proponents of Taiwan independence. Lee Teng-hui, however, gradually abolished the blacklist system and the use of legal means against independence activists. While KMT members surrounding Hau Pei-tsun favored a 'one China' policy, opposed the democratization of Taiwan, and proposed a strong cabinet system of government, Lee Teng-hui pursued policies aiming in just the opposite direction. The New KMT Alliance that spearheaded the non-mainstream faction split off from the KMT and formed the New Party in 1993 (Chu and Lin, 1996: 84-5; Cheng and Hsu, 1996: 151-2).

After the nomination of Lien Chan as the KMT candidate for the 2000 Presidential election, James Soong (Song Chu-yu), who was deeply disappointed for not being nominated, run as independent candidate and, one day thereafter, announced the formation of a new party. As a consequence, the KMT has to deal with another large break-off party, the People First Party (PFP).

The latest development that has a tremendous effect on the KMT is the full public support of former President Lee Teng-hui for the Taiwan Solidarity Union (TSU). Lee, though holding no post within the new party, has formed an important think tank organization, the Taiwan Advocates – that stands close to the TSU – where he is exercising direct influence on a large number of prominent, mostly former KMT politicians. On September 21, 2001, Lee was expelled from the KMT for openly endorsing the TSU (cf M.C. Lin, 2001b; Low, 2001). In fact, Lee tries to tear apart pro-Mainland oriented KMT members led by Ma Ying-jiou, Chu Li-lun and Jason Hu from pro-local oriented ones (most of whom are in the parliament), such as Wang Jin-pyn, the speaker of the legislature (cf C.Y. Lin, 2001). Lee said to KMT lawmakers that if they were interested, they could join the Taiwan Advocates or the TSU (M.C. Lin, 2001a).

With regard to social policy, the KMT – a through and through conservative party – resorted to a very pragmatic social policy stance in the 1990s. While showing a general reluctance of introducing new social policies, the KMT resorted to expensive social policy program as a means to win elections, such as universal old-age allowances. Lee Teng-hui was the architect of these new policies and, after his leaving the KMT, the social policies pursued by Lee are at risk.

The Democratic Progressive Party

History and Development Though being established only in 1986, the history of the DPP and its predecessor, the Dangwai (meaning 'outside the party') movement, goes back to the mid-1970s. Besides the ruling KMT and two tiny fraternal parties – the China Youth Party and the China Democratic Socialist Party – no other political parties were allowed. Nonetheless, on the contrary to many other authoritarian regimes, the KMT allowed the participation of non-party candidates in local elections. The tradition of independent non-party candidates joining elections enabled the DPP to form its political network long before the formal establishment of the party.

In the mid-1970s, the opposition movement gathered momentum and started to build up a nationwide network of political alliances, thus connecting the political activities of the opposition movement in local elections districts (Tien, 1996: 10). In the 1977 elections for the Provincial Assembly and county magistrates, the opposition movement won its first important electoral victory since 21 opposition candidates were elected to the Provincial Assembly and four were elected to county magistrates. This victory encouraged some opposition leaders to take a more radical anti-government line (Wu, 1995: 90).

Over the next two years, two ideologically distinct camps crystallized in the opposition movement. The one, under the leadership of Huang Hsin-chieh, tried to reform the political system as a whole ('gai ge ti zhi') and the other, under the leadership of Kang Ning-hsiang, to reform the system from within ('ti zhi nei gai ge'). In 1979 each of these groups launched its own magazine. The *Formosa* magazine published by Huang Hsin-chieh was much more radical than *The Eighties* published by Kang Ning-hsiang and, therefore, it was closed by the Taiwan Garrison Command after having only published four issues.

On December 10, 1979, the Formosa faction organized a rally for the cause of the Human Rights Day. Public speeches were held by leading activists of the Formosa group that heavily criticized the ruling KMT. Though sixty activists were jailed and eight of them, all leading figures of the Formosa group, were subsequently tried in the military tribunal on charges of sedition and sentenced to prison terms of twelve to fourteen years, except for She Ming-teh who was given a life term (Jiang and Wu, 1992: 87), the Kaohsiung Incident marked a new beginning rather than the end of the Formosa group and the DPP.

Non-party candidates in the following elections had to promise not to advocate or support either communism or the Taiwan Independence movement, and not to state that they were representing those in jail as a result of the Kaohsiung Incident. In turn, the government informally guaranteed to control or, if necessary, suppress KMT-loyal veterans or other groups that might interfere with the activities of non-party candidates and to order the police organization to protect and not in any way harass independent candidates (cf Copper, 1981a: 378).

In the 1980 Legislative Yuan, the Dangwai movement won 8.28 percent of votes respectively which added up to six seats in the Legislative Yuan, i.e. 8.7 percent of the 69 seats to be elected. Some wives of imprisoned opposition leaders joined the elections and continued successfully the struggle of the opposition movement. In the subsequent years, the share of overall Dangwai (the precursor of the DPP) votes rose to 16.68 percent in 1983, and 22.22 percent in 1986 (Hu and Chu, 1992: 183-5). The showdown of military regime in the aftermath of the Kaohsiung Incident, thus, ended in a triumph of the opposition movement, and not in the defeat of it.

In spring of 1984, those Dangwai activists who held elective offices formed the Association of Public Policy Studies as the coordination center of their movement, which set up branch offices all over the island. Though the Democratic Progressive Party was formed on September 28, in 1986. Martial law was lifted only the following year, on July 15, and the full recognition of new political parties were only to come in January, 1989, with the enactment of the Law for Civic Organizations (Jiang and Wu, 1992: 86-7). The Democratic Progressive Party had been established under the leadership of wives and lawyers who, in the meantime, were elected to public offices, as the important members of the opposition movement still had to serve their terms as political prisoners. Not only the first chairman of the DPP, Jiang Peng-jian, was one of the lawyers who defended those arrested in the Kaohsiung Incident, but also a whole new generation of DPP leaders, among which were, for example, Chen Shui-bian (future Taipei mayor, and President), Hsieh Chang-ting (future Kaohsiung mayor and DPP chairman), and Su Zhen-chang (future Taipei county commissioner).

A new group of leaders emerged from among assistants to first generation DPP leaders that were elected to public offices centering around their founding magazine New Tide ('Xin Chao Liu'). This new group of

DPP leaders has established the New Tide faction. Though numerically being a minority group, the New Tide faction soon became indispensable to DPP as it held a sizable power base in social organizations supporting socially disadvantaged or excluded groups. From the establishment of the New Tide faction in 1987 to the present, the generation and ideology gap between the Formosa faction and the New Tide faction makes up the major divide in DPP party politics. The New Tide faction heavily promoted the cause of Taiwan independence.

The DPP, on the contrary to the KMT, could prevent the break-off of a major party faction that, thus, could form a new party (Cheng and Hsu, 1996). The KMT lost three major factions who formed their own parties, the New Party, the People First Party and the Taiwan Solidarity Union, all of which significantly reduced the electorate of the KMT and its political weight. The DPP, on the contrary, experienced the formation of only minor break-away parties, i.e. the Labor Party, the Workers Party, the Chinese Social Democratic Party, the Green Party, the New Nation Alliance, and the Taiwan Independence Party, which did not harm the overall power base of the DPP. Instead, the formation of these new parties led to an increased cohesion of the leading party ideology and the party elite. In case, the New Tide faction would have left the party, the DPP would have lost large shares of its active members and an important share of its electorate.

Without the integration of the New Tide faction into policymaking of the DPP, the development of the DPP would have certainly gone into another direction. The New Tide 'had come close to exercising the option of leaving the party' for several times in the 1980s (ibid.: 138). The most important question for the development of the DPP, thus, is: How did the DPP manage to maintain elite cohesion within the DPP? Why did the leading Formosa faction agree to take in the goal of Taiwan independence into the party program, and not risk the exit of the New Tide faction?

First, the New Tide faction already has a high degree of internal organization, a widespread network of service centers around the island, and a sound financial basis as elected New Tide members have to turn in their whole salary and to live on salaries as service center activists. In addition, New Tide served as a reception camp for a large number of former members of the Formosa faction that have left their faction on their own or with the help of their other faction members, or faction members that have been alienated from the Formosa faction.

A number of core Formosa leaders in the past have been supported by the New Tide, such as Yao Chia-wen, Lin Yi-hsiung and She Ming-teh (who is often referred to Taiwan's Nelson Mandela, for he was 25 years imprisoned). All of them became chairmen of the DPP with the help of the New Tide faction. Second, the radical Taiwan Independence stand of the

New Tide faction could be accepted by the Formosa faction because both recruited their voters from the sub-ethnic group that forms the majority of the Taiwanese population, 'Minnan Ren' (who speak the local Taiwanese, i.e. Minnan Chinese); but also from the Hakka[16] minority.

This second determinant differentiates the cases of internal party cleavages between factions of the DPP and the KMT. In the 1990s, the mainstream faction of the KMT around Lee Teng-hui relied, to an overwhelming extent, on the votes of the Taiwanese, on the contrary to the non-mainstream faction. Hence, the KMT did not accept to retreat to a strict One-China-policy as it feared to loose support of the masses. In fact, the KMT mainstream faction and the Formosa faction had a similar stand on the Independence-Unification issue. But, after the incorporation of a more radical Taiwan Independence goal into the DPP party program in October 1991, the KMT found itself in a precarious situation. While the hardliners from the non-mainstream KMT faction demanded the severe punishment and the extinction of DPP activists, the mainstream faction began to distance itself from the traditional One-China policy and tried to adapt it to Taiwan's reality.

When the non-mainstream members had lost all their major battles and saw that they were excluded from powerful posts inside the KMT and the government whereas the members of the Collective Wisdom Club has risen to power within the KMT, they had no other choice than to quit the KMT and to form the New Party (Huang, 1996: 126-7). The formation of the second and third break-off parties from the KMT (i.e. PFP and TSU) followed the same pattern: exclusion from power positions, intense personal fights and, most importantly, a disagreement on the future of Taiwan, i.e. the Independence/Localization versus Unification issue. The DPP, on the contrary to the KMT, has survived all major changes, and formation of factions within its own ranks; largely by incorporation of new developments and by avoiding exclusion of representatives of new factions from powerful positions within the DPP.

The Formosa faction of the DPP managed to integrate the New Tide faction into the DPP; to accept its ideology and, most importantly, to share power positions. In alternating way, the post of the DPP chairperson went to a chairperson supported by the New Tide faction and then, a chairperson supported by the Formosa faction. Yao Chia-wen had become the second chairman of the DPP; She Ming-teh the sixth, and Lin Yi-hsiung the eighth chairman of the DPP (see App. 1.2).

Factions and Policies Throughout most of its history, the DPP had been divided into two major, dominant factions at a time. These factions sprang up from the editorial staff of party magazines, for example, *Formosa*, *The*

Eighties, *China Tide*, *Progress*, and *New Tide*. In the beginning, the opposition movement of the Dangwai consisted of two factions, the Formosa faction and the Kang faction, with Huang Hsin-chieh and Kang Ning-hsiang as their respective leaders. During the second half of the 1970s, both factions developed within the Dangwai movement. The Formosa faction was very radical and tried to provoke, and overthrow the ruling administration with street protests and mass mobilization. The Kang faction, on the contrary, adhered to moderate means of political agitation, such as electoral contest for public offices that were to be elected by the people and political protest within elected bodies in town, city and county councils; the Provincial and National Assemblies; and the Legislative Yuan.

The KMT regime was not opposed to Kang, and in 1986, Kang could celebrate a big victory as he won the second highest number of votes in the Legislative Yuan elections island-wide. After 1987, the Kang faction was subject to intense isolation from two other factions that now became the dominant forces within the DPP, the Formosa and the New Tide faction. In December 1988, owing to the growing isolation within the DPP, a founding member of the Kang faction, Fei Hsi-ping, who was a Mainland-elected member of the Legislative Yuan left the DPP in order to protest planned, forced retirement of all Legislative Yuan and National Assembly delegates that were elected on the mainland (Long, 1991: 195). This forced retirement cost Fei his job but opened the DPP vast new opportunities of gaining a great number of seats in the two houses of parliament. What followed next was the dissolution of the Kang faction; its members joined other minor groups that existed in the DPP outside the Formosa and the New Tide factions.

The Formosa faction survived due to the efforts of the family members of those leaders arrested following the Kaohsiung Incident in 1979, since they participated in elections in their place. By 1987, the Formosa faction had been reformed and followed a much more moderate policy stance, i.e. promoting political change via participation in democratic elections and, once elected, via policymaking in elected governmental bodies. The Formosa faction adopted a liberal democratic, but still very conservative policy stance with regard to economic and social policy issues, such as being supportive to free trade with Mainland China, health insurance and old-age pensions; and being reluctant regarding unemployment insurance and a rise of taxes in order to finance social policy and welfare programs (TAO, 1997).

Since 1980, in the aftermath of the Kaohsiung Incident, two new factions evolved, which, however, were of lesser importance. One was formed by young intellectuals who served as assistants to those holding elected posts, and as editors of their magazines. One of these magazines was *Plow Deep*, the magazine of Hsu Jung-su, the wife of imprisoned Chang Chun-hung (Arrigo, 1994: 161). Having been denied the recognition of their work and access to higher positions within the DPP, these intellectuals gradually formed a new movement, which was transformed into a distinction party faction in 1987 with the foundation of the New Tide faction. The New Tide faction, on the contrary to the Formosa faction, has a very high degree of discipline among its members, as well as a high degree of autonomy from the central party headquarter. The New Tide faction can rely on an independent network of offices of New Tide members who got elected for a public office and local service centers of grass root organizations.

The second faction that emerged in the early eighties was the Progress faction who distinguished itself from the New Tide activists by pursuing a pro-unification policy. Both the New Tide and the Progress faction upheld the ideas of social democracy and resorted to the means of street protest and mass mobilization. As the Progress faction that was led by a Mainlander grassroots reformer, Lin Cheng-jie, rejected the Independence policy of the New Tide faction, it joined the Formosa faction in 1988 that supported self-determination policy instead (Cheng and Hsu, 1996: 144-5, 150).

The Independence versus Unification issue also split off another faction that directly emerged out of the New Tide movement, i.e. the China Tide faction. The China Tide faction was composed of a few leftist intellectuals who called for working-class mobilization and aspired the unification of Taiwan and Mainland China. In 1987, leaders of the China Tide faction quit the DPP and formed the Labor Party ('Gong Dang'), a faction of which formed the more radical Workers Party ('Lao Dong Dang') one year later.

With the rise of independent politicians inside the DPP who could count own means to win elections, usually fame and a great number of financial supporters, new factions evolved in the 1990s. The two leading figures that lead these factions are Chen Shui-bian and Hsieh Chang-ting, both were among the lawyers who defended the eight Formosa leaders who were accused of sedition in front the military tribunal in 1979. The newly formed factions were the Justice Alliance faction and the Welfare State faction, which formed a 'centrist' party platform that could mediate between the New Tide and the Formosa factions. Pertaining to social policy, the leaders of both factions, Chen Shui-bian and Hsieh Chang-ting, advanced a mixture of liberal democratic and social democratic policy stand.

The new President of Taiwan, Chen Shui-bian, proposes a more soft policy stand towards the People's Republic of China on the issue of cross-strait relations, as well as an active pro-business stand, both comparable to that of the Formosa faction. Chen Shui-bian, the former Taipei mayor, had his independent headquarters – from where he runs the elections and the business of the Justice Alliance faction – in Taipei; and Hsieh Chang-ting, the Kaoshiung mayor, had his Welfare State faction headquarters in Kaoshiung.

In 1999, the old Formosa faction began to split into the New Era Institute faction ('Xin Shi Ji') and the New Dynamic faction ('Xin Dong Li'). The New Era Institute faction was set up by Chang Chun-hung who was a leading member of the Formosa faction from the very beginning. The leader of the New Dynamic faction is Chen Zhong-xin (cf Table 2). The old Formosa Faction recently lost a good deal of support within the party; now, there is only one member left in the 31-member-strong central committee of the DPP.

Chen Shui-bian's Justice Alliance turned into the new Mainstream Alliance, 'Zhu Liu Lian Meng'. The new Mainstream Alliance also recruited a lot of members from the Welfare State faction, the Justice faction, and Taiwan Independence Alliance (the leader of which is Li Ying-yuan). The Mainstream Alliance and the New Tide Faction are now the two key players inside the DPP (cf SCH, 2002; Chen, 2001).

Besides these factions at central party level, there are also a large number of local factions that help to determine election results a great deal (cf Jacobs, 2001), but these have not yet determined the fate of the DPP itself. Party factions within the DPP rely on their own human and financial resources, and thus, enjoy a high degree of independence within the organization of the DPP. In recent years, these factions had been strengthened by the charisma and the fast growing fame of their leaders, especially Chen Shui-bian and Hsieh Chang-ting.

The New Party

Members of the non-mainstream faction of the KMT formed the New KMT Alliance (a party faction) in 1990, and a new party, the New Party (NP), in 1993. There leaders were Zhao Shao-kang, former head of the Environmental Protection Agency of the central government, and Wang Jian-xuan, former finance minister. The main theme of their political agenda was the fight against money politics and political corruption. On the contrary to most KMT candidates, Zhao's and Wang's name remained unsullied in the years they served as members of the government. Thus, they successfully launched a new campaign against the dirty politics of the mainstream KMT.

The New Party emerged out of the New KMT Alliance who chalked up a considerable success in the 1992 Legislative elections. The non-mainstream faction won 25 seats with only having 26 candidates nominated, thus, making the non-mainstream faction a de facto party in 1992 (Lin and Zhang, 1998: 135-6). The isolation of the New KMT Alliance and their exclusion from power with the government and the party forced the split with the KMT in summer 1993. In city mayor and county commissioner elections of the same year, in two counties, the New Party won a considerable share of votes, e.g. 16.3 percent in Taipei county and 10.1 percent in Hsinchu City.

The success story of the New Party was limited from the very beginning. The New Party mainly competed for votes of the Mainlander electorate as well as the sizeable part of the electorate who had one or the other relatives who were coming from the mainland; there had been many mixed marriages (e.g. up to one fourth of the population in Taipei). Most of the voters who voted for the New Party were members of the new middle class. These voters lived and work in central urban areas, and their parents (at least one of them) were former KMT officials and soldiers that fled to Taiwan in 1949.

In 1994 election for the Taipei mayor, the New Party received its largest share of votes in elections ever, i.e. a little less than one third of total votes; having made it an equally powerful party beside the KMT and the DPP on city council level the next four years. In the 1998 Legislative Yuan elections, the New Party gained 7.06 percent of votes and 4.89 percent of seats. Therefore, the New Party has been able to hold, together with other minor parties and independent MPs and, since the year 2000, also the PFP, the balance of power. In 2001, the December 1 parliamentary elections, however, meant a final blow to the success story of the New Party, turning it into a rather insignificant political player, winning 2.86 percent of votes (Yeh, 2001).

The People First Party

After having joined the Presidential election as an independent candidate, James Soong was expelled from the KMT. Usually in Taiwan politics, such as attempt is doomed to fail, since party support is most vital for winning elections in Taiwan, especially in a winner-takes-all election, such as the Presidential election. James Soong was a political heavyweight for a long time by then. When serving as Provincial Governor of Taiwan Province (i.e. Taiwan and the Pescadores without its two major cities, Taipei and Kaohsiung, which are placed right under the rule of the Central government), James Soong managed to build up his own political empire with intensive use of the abundant funding of the Provincial government for building strong relationships with local leaders all around the island.

James Soong, for this reason, could count on the support of a great number of local KMT factions.

The financial patronage system towards helping local factions that were loyal to him paid off in the end. Then, in the year 2000, Soong easily won 4.66 million votes without the help of a party organization, solely relying on his charisma as a political strongman and the strong support of a great number of local KMT factions. He almost came across snatching the presidency from Chen Shui-bian. Almost no Mainlander, or Mainland-oriented voters has voted for Lien Chan in the Presidential election, causing Lien to return to a China stance and to abandon Lee's 'nativization' policy later on (cf Lee, 2001). But, the PFP continues to be tremendously popular among this voter segment, but the PFP also tries to catch the vote of Taiwan-oriented voters. In the 2001 Parliamentary elections, the PFP won 20.34 percent of votes, leading to 46 seats in parliament; making it the third strongest party in Taiwan – the DPP and the KMT won 35.65 and 31.28 percent, i.e. 87 and 68 seats, respectively (Yeh, 2001).

Soong's People First Party is a rather conservative party. Besides its policy of long-term, peaceful unification with Mainland China, the party also pursues a clear economy-first policy, and prefers limited and targeted social policies for the most needy groups of people.

The Taiwan Solidarity Union

Among today's major parties of the Taiwan political landscape only the Taiwan Solidarity Union uses Taiwan in its name. Lee Teng-hui said that 'only this party can fight for Taiwan's future' (Lin and Ide, 2001). Lee wants to launch a reform of all major political parties in Taiwan by promoting the cause of the Taiwan Solidarity Union and vows to 'eliminate those parties which are not focused on Taiwan', obviously referring to the New Party and also remaining China-orientated circles in the KMT (ibid.).

The ultimate goal for the TSU and Lee Teng-hui's efforts is to stabilize the political situation of Taiwan under Chen Shui-bian, since KMT and ex-KMT forces in the parliament – that, together, are still holding a majority of seats – tend to blockade rather than cooperate with the new government and the President, which was and is not good for the future of Taiwan (cf Tzou, 2001).

Huang Chu-wen, former Minister of Interior, formed a new political group, which – later on – became the TSU, in order to 'permit a more efficient DPP governance and maintain Lee's Taiwan First legacy'. Huang helped Lee to establish the Collective Wisdom Club in 1988, and believed in Lee from the very beginning, at a time when Lee's power base was still very shaky (Hsu, 2001).

With the New Tide faction becoming stronger inside the DPP, the TSU might well compete for the same voter segment, since both advance a clear pro-Taiwan policy stance.

But, the promise of the TSU to cooperate with the DPP, and the open policy of recruiting Taiwan-oriented KMT politicians, rather serves the DPP than does any harm to it. Most, TSU supporters are from the countryside, and again from Southern Taiwan. The more ex-KMT legislators join the TSU, the more it will be clear that they attract voters of the traditional KMT electorate, and not that of the DPP. Winning 8.5 percent of votes and 13 seats in the 2001 parliamentary elections, the TSU now plays a vital role in supporting the power base of the DPP, since both parties together now hold 100 parliamentary seats out of 225 total seats (Yeh, 2001).

Table 2: Major Parties/Factions and their Stance in Social Policy

Party/Faction	Political doctrine	Priority	Leaders
KMT – mainstream	conservative	economy first	Lien Chan
New Party	conservative	economy first	Wang Jian-xuan
People First Party	conservative	economy first	James Soong
Taiwan Solidarity Union	conservative	economy first	Huang Chu-wen
DPP – New Era Institute faction	liberal democratic	economy first	Chang Chun-hung
DPP – New Dynamic faction	liberal democratic	economy first	Hsieh Chang-ting
DPP – Mainstream Alliance	liberal/social democratic	balanced	Chen Shui-bian
DPP – New Tide faction	social democratic	social welfare first	Wu Nai-ren, Qiu Yi-ren

Sources: www.dpp.org.tw; www.taipeitimes.com.tw; Huang (2001a); and SCH (2002).

4 The Development of the Taiwanese Welfare State

The Social Insurance System

The Labor Insurance Scheme

In 1950, the Kuomintang government implemented the Regulations Governing the Taiwan Labor Insurance, which created the Labor Insurance scheme under the administration of the Provincial Government. This was the first step in putting the constitutional provision for the introduction of a social insurance system (C, Art. 155) into practice. The new Labor Insurance scheme covered a wide range of social risks, such as maternity, injury and illness, disability, old age, and death. The scheme provided exclusively cash benefit payments. With the introduction of the medical benefit for industrial workers in 1956, the scheme also provided in-kind benefits in form of free hospitalization treatment (BLI, 1997). The Labor Insurance scheme allowed industrial workers both employed by the government and private factories and mines with more than 20 workers to join the governmental labor insurance scheme.

The period from 1950 to the year 1958, the year in that the Labor Insurance Law has been put into effect, was a testing period in which the government gradually extended the coverage of this insurance scheme. The long period reserved for testing the new scheme unveils the deep-seated worries of the KMT regime, which principally opposed the implementation of social insurance schemes that increased the cost of labor. In 1951, the coverage has been extended to include workers in private factories employing ten employees and over (H.S. Chan, 1985: 326). In the same year, craft workers were also allowed to join the scheme with the implementation of the Regulations Governing the Taiwan Craft Workers. In following years, the government also incorporated fishery workers (1953) and sugarcane farmers (1956). On July 21, 1958, the Legislative Yuan passed the Labor Insurance Act (CLA, 1997), with which it transformed the Labor Insurance into a statutory insurance scheme. From then on, the Central Government, took over the administration of the scheme; thus, turning the Labor Insurance into a national scheme (BLI, 1997; H.S. Chan, 1985: 326).

In 1960, medical benefits were extended to all societal groups that have joined the Labor Insurance scheme by then. In 1965, manual workers, drivers and mechanics employed by governmental agencies and public schools were also approved to join the Labor Insurance scheme. In 1970, the range of benefits under the scheme was extended to include outpatient treatment as well. The amendment of the Labor Insurance Act of the same year broadened the compulsory coverage of the scheme so that it included manual workers and staff members working in commercial firms and shops, ranches, and pastures that employed ten or more workers. In addition, journalists, cultural workers, private school teachers and staff members, as well as employees of cooperatives and nonprofit organizations, civic bodies and department stores, from then on, could join the scheme on a voluntary basis (BLI, 1997).

In 1979, the amendments of the Labor Insurance Act extended the compulsory coverage of the scheme a great deal: first, its coverage was extended to all workers in private firms with more than five employees (H.S. Chan, 1985: 327) and, second, those who were allowed to join the scheme on a voluntary basis before, i.e. staff employed by governmental agencies and public schools under contract; employees in journalistic, cultural, nonprofit organizations and cooperative enterprise; as well as skilled workers receiving practical training, now were subject to compulsory participation in the scheme. In addition, workers formerly outside the scope of the Labor Insurance Act could join the scheme on an optional basis. The 1979 amendment liberalized the eligibility requirements and provided more generous benefits to members of the Labor Insurance scheme. The 1988 amendments of the Labor Insurance Act required full-time employed fishermen to join the scheme through their fishing company. These amendments also liberalized the eligibility requirements and provided more generous benefits to the members of the Labor Insurance scheme (BLI, 1997).

Table 3 shows the development of membership of the Labor Insurance scheme, as well as that of due premiums and total benefits granted. In the first three decades of the Labor Insurance scheme, premium payments exceeded paid benefits a great deal, i.e. on an average by 38.19 percent. In the early 1980s, the amount of outgoing payments surpassed for the first time that of overall premiums paid. In the consecutive years of 1985, 1986 and 1987, premium payments had been constantly below benefits. But thereafter, premiums payments increased again a great deal. A look at the membership numbers of the Labor Insurance scheme in Table 5 tells us that a hefty continuous increase in the membership – 9.15 percent on average per year from 1979 to 1994 – brought about the increase in the total amount of premiums. From 1995 onwards, the amount of benefits paid to the insured had been decreasing mainly due to a decline in membership of the labor insurance program. Regarding the contributions paid it needs to be said that laborers bore 20 percent of premiums, and the employer 80 percent; the self-employed had to pay 60 percent themselves and the government contributed 40 percent (Chang, 1998: 34).

Table 3: The Development of Labor Insurance

Year	No. of Persons Insured	Annual Increase/Decrease in Membership in percent	Due Premium in million Taiwan dollar (TWD)	Total Benefits Paid in million TWD
1950-1979	2,283,516	-	35,249	25,507
1980	2,538,125	11.15	10,182	8,859
1981	2,781,512	9.59	13,379	12,552
1982	2,950,119	6.06	15,342	15,445
1983	3,322,977	12.64	18,386	17,772
1984	3,693,276	11.14	23,912	22,697
1985	4,049,472	9.64	28,175	29,312
1986	4,711,969	16.36	32,422	34,782
1987	5,321,733	12.94	39,127	41,418
1988	5,980,157	12.37	48,389	45,464
1989	6,549,661	9.52	61,024	53,112
1990	6,852,978	4.63	72,999	61,172
1991	7,281,445	6.25	86,453	79,217
1992	7,708,868	5.87	104,205	92,837
1993	8,144,183	5.64	123,089	105,859
1994	8,496,883	4.33	138,456	129,432
1995	7,635,063	-10.14	134,902	108,598
1996	7,434,299	-2.63	129,408	70,461

Source: Bureau of Labor Insurance (1997), 'Yearbook of Labor Insurance Statistics', pp. 14-5.

When looking at the structural composition of benefits granted under the Labor Insurance scheme, we see that between 1950 and 1996 24.24 percent of all Labor Insurance benefits were old-age benefit payments (Table 4). The second most important item among the different kinds of benefits was death benefit payments to dependents of the deceased. Maternity benefit payments added up to 6.47 percent, while benefits for injury, illness and disabilities were negligible, amounting to 3.72 percent of overall benefits. During the same period, medical benefit payments made up 51.01 percent of total benefits, with outpatient benefit payments being clearly higher than inpatient benefit payments, 31.59 to 19.42 percent of total benefit payments.

The special feature of the Taiwanese social security system – of which the sole major column until 1995 was the Labor Insurance system – is the relative insignificance of social assistance benefits. These were, above all, benefits for illness, injury, disability and unemployment; but also costly inpatient and outpatient health care services.

Table 4: Benefits of Labor Insurance (1950-1996)

Type of Benefit	1950-1996		
	No. of Claims in thousand	Amount in mill. TWD	Amount in percent
Grand total	*1,064,166*	*951,277*	*100*
Total cash benefit payments	*11,107*	*466,099*	*48,99*
Maternity benefit payments	5,474	61,609	6.47
Injury or illness benefit payments	3,043	12,514	1.32
Disability benefit payments	259	22,822	2.40
Old-age benefit payments	839	230,633	24.24
Death benefit payments	1,491	138,519	14.56
Total medical benefit payments	*1,053,058*	*485,177*	*51.01*
Inpatient benefit payments	9,629	184,724	19.42
Outpatient benefit payments	1,043,428	300,453	31.59

Note: The real numbers for occupational injury medical insurance since March 1995 are not included. Until 1994, only the due numbers (not the real numbers) of claims of inpatient and outpatient benefit payments had been counted. The differences in the number of claims and the amount caused hereby are minor ones.

Source: Bureau of Labor Insurance (1997), 'Yearbook of Labor Insurance Statistics', p. 18.

When compared to the structure of labor insurance benefits in 1996 (Table 5), we note a sizeable increase in the level of benefits going to the disabled, which may be directly explained by the success of the disabled welfare movements in the late 1980s and early 1990s (Hsiao, 2001). Old-age benefits heave increased a good deal in importance due to rapid ageing of the Taiwanese society, augmenting to about 61 percent of non-medical care benefits in 1996, which represented 99.98 of all benefits after the transfer of medical benefits to the new health insurance system.

Table 5: Benefits of Labor Insurance (1996)

Type of Benefit	1996		
	No. of Claims in thousand	Amount in mill. TWD	Amount in percent
Grand total	*562*	*68,898*	*100*
Total cash benefit payments	*549*	*68,883*	*99.98*
Maternity benefit payments	180	3,557	5.16
Injury or illness benefit payments	149	1,329	1.93
Disability benefit payments	17	3,654	5.30
Old-age benefit payments	108	41,746	60.59
Death benefit payments	92	18,596	27.00
Total medical benefit payments	*12.9*	*14.5*	*0.02*
Inpatient benefit payments	0.2	6.7	0.01
Outpatient benefit payments	12.7	7.8	0.01

Note: The real number for occupational injury medical insurance is not included.
Source: Bureau of Labor Insurance (1997), 'Yearbook of Labor Insurance Statistics', p. 19.

In 1996, the Bureau of Labor Insurance for the Taiwan-Fujian Area had been renamed into Bureau of Labor Insurance and subordinated to the Council of Labor Affairs of the Central Government. Subsequently, a Labor Insurance Supervisory Commission has been set up to deliberate insurance disputes and to supervise the operations of the Labor Insurance. The composition of this commission displays a four-fold structure, as memberships are equally divided among representatives of relevant government agencies, representatives of laborers, representatives of employers and insurance specialists (BLI, 1997).

Social Insurance Schemes for Military Servicemen

Half a year after the retreat from Mainland China, the government implemented a new social insurance scheme for the military personnel, the Servicemen Insurance Plan, in June 1950. The benefits of the new insurance scheme included death allowance and three kinds of disability allowances. The servicemen had to come up for 35 percent of contributions, the rest was paid by the government; soldiers, however, did not need to pay anything, the government took over responsibility for paying for all their insurance fees. Three years later the Insurance Provisions for Army, Navy, and Air Force Servicemen had been promulgated, which had been revised in 1956. In 1970, the government yet again revised the regulations for insurance of its military personnel and implemented the Servicemen Insurance Provisions (Chang, 1998: 34-5; Chan and Yang, 2001; CEPD, 1996).

The Insurance Schemes for Employees and their Dependents of Government Organizations and Private Schools

In January 1958, the government promulgated the Government Employees' Insurance Law in order to 'protect the livelihood of civil servants, to enhance their welfare so as to increase their working efficiency' (CTC, 1997: 3). The Government Employees' Insurance scheme was operated by the Central Trust of China under the supervision of the Ministry of Personnel of the ROC. The Government Employees' Insurance provided medical care benefits for maternity, sickness, injury; cash benefits for maternity, sickness, injury; cash benefits for disability, old age, death and dependents' funeral allowance. In June 1961, the government established the Government Employees' Insurance Department. The Government Employees' Insurance also incorporated the spouses and dependents of the insured. The premium rate for the insured was 35 percent and for the government 65 percent (Hwang and Hill, 1997: 80; Chang, 1998: 35). In August 1965, the government set up the Retired Government Employees' Insurance scheme that should extend coverage to retired employees.

For keeping pace with the increasing demand for benefits of the Government Employment Insurance program, the Parliament amended in January 1974 the Government Employee Insurance Law to introduce a flexible premium rate system, adjusting the original premium rate 7 percent of the insured's monthly salary to a range between 7 and 9 percent. The

Central Trust of China decided, however, not to increase the original rate of 7 percent for the next few years in order to prevent an increase in the financial burden of the insured. The inevitable deficit of the Government Employment Insurance eventually caused an increase of the premium rate by one percentage point in July 1977 and again another increase of one percentage point in August 1980. In the early 1980s, the government enacted a law for a new Health Insurance for Government Employees' Dependents program as an additional effort to increase government employees' social security provision.

The new scheme started to operate in July 1982. In the beginning, the new health insurance scheme only covered the spouses of government employees. The initial premium rate of 3 percent was paid half-and-half by the insured and the government. In June 1977 the government introduced differential rates for government employees and retired government employees respectively, keeping the premium rate for retirees at a constant 8 percent, which they had to pay entirely by themselves. In addition, the government also set up a Health Insurance for Retired Government Employees and a Health Insurance for Spouses of Retired Government Employees in July 1985. The premium rate of these two new schemes was 9 percent, the burden of which was carried by the government and the insured to equal parts (CTC, 1997).

In August 1980, the government entrusted the Central Trust of China with the operation of a new Insurance for Teaching and Administrative Staff of Private Schools in August 1980. The new insurance scheme started to operate only two months later. In January 1984, the government came up with a new idea of implementing an additional insurance scheme for retired teaching and administrative staff of private schools. Its premium rate, medicine care and cash benefits were the same as those of the Retired Government Employees Insurance scheme. Only one and a half years later, in July 1985, the government created two new health insurance schemes, the Health Insurance for Spouses of Retired Teaching and Administrative Staff of Private Schools and the Health Insurance for Retired Teaching and Administrative Staff of Private Schools. These new schemes resembled the health insurance schemes of retired government employees and the spouses, which were enacted on the same day. The premium rate was set at 9 percent and it was shared equally by the government and the retired staff of private schools. The Insurance for Teaching and Administrative Staff of Private Schools stopped operating, for all its insured persons have been switched to participate in the health insurance for retired teaching and administrative staff of private schools.

Throughout the 1980s and 1990s, the premium rates for the Retired Government Employees' Insurance remained 8 percent in consideration of the lack of earnings of the insured and their full premium payment. The coverage of the Health Insurance for Government Employees' Dependents was extended to parents and unmarried disabled children in 1989 and 1991 respectively. The original premium rate of 3 percent was increased to 5 percent. After the introduction of the National Health Insurance in 1995, the administration of medical care benefits was transferred to the Bureau of the National Health Insurance. The Government Employees' Insurance Department continued to implement the enrollment and cash benefits provided by the insurance program (CTC, 1997).

In January, 1990, a new health insurance scheme, the Health Insurance for Retired Teaching and Administrative Staff of Private Schools, was set up to include spouses retired teaching and administrative staff of private schools. The scheme had been extended to parents in November 1991. Still, in July 1992, the government also incorporated in this new health insurance scheme unmarried children of the insured. At the beginning, the premium rate was set at 5 percent and, then, reduced to 3.8 percent of which the insured had to pay 50 percent, the school 25 percent and the government the remaining 25 percent.

Just a couple of months before the implementation of the National Health Insurance Act in July 1994, the government decided to modify the structure health insurance schemes for retired employees and their dependents of both government organizations and private schools by unifying them into a single system. The Central Trust of China emphasized the new simplicity of the new system; the improvement of the financial structure and the widened risk pooling that has been achieved by this reform. The Statute of Health Insurance for Retired Government Employees was transformed into the Statute of Health Insurance for Retired Employees and Their Dependents of Government Organizations and Private Schools (HIREDGOPS) on March 28, 1994. All the insured of the Health Insurance for Retired Government Employees, the Health Insurance for Spouses of Retired Government Employees, the Health Insurance for Retired Teaching and Administrative Staff of Private Schools, Health Insurance for Spouses of Retired Teaching and Administrative Staff of Private Schools were allocated to the newly created health insurance scheme. After the implementation of the National Health Insurance in March 1995, the administration of medical care benefits of employees and their dependents of private schools had been also transferred to the Bureau of National Health Insurance. All former occupationally divided health insurance schemes had been ceased (CTC, 1997).

The membership numbers of social insurance schemes for government employees and employees of private schools throughout the years (see Tables 6 to 9) display a rather continuous increase.

Table 6: Development of Membership of Government Employee Insurance (GEI) and Retired Government Employee Insurance (RGEI), in persons

Year	All schemes for staff of gov't units and private schools	GEI Gov't Employee Insurance			RGEI Retired Gov't Employee Insurance		
		Total	Central Gov't	Local Gov't	Total	Central Gov't	Local Gov't
1958	172,469	172,469	28,723	143,746	-	-	-
1959	189,271	189,271	35,377	153,894	-	-	-
1960	203,909	203,909	42,513	161,396	-	-	-
1961	213,419	213,419	44,722	168,697	-	-	-
1962	218,434	218,434	45,611	172,823	-	-	-
1963	224,743	224,743	46,528	178,215	-	-	-
1964	232,262	232,262	47,845	184,417	-	-	-
1965	241,955	240,261	50,834	189,427	1,694	607	1,087
1966	250,155	247,257	52,452	194,805	2,898	856	2,042
1967	259,133	255,923	55,289	200,634	3,210	967	2,243
1968	271,145	267,328	59,476	207,852	3,817	1,167	2,650
1969	282,845	278,222	63,336	214,886	4,623	1,493	3,130
1970	298,667	293,531	68,604	224,927	5,136	1,601	3,535
1971	313,106	307,403	75,045	232,358	5,703	1,756	3,947
1972	329,016	322,615	79,619	242,996	6,401	2,195	4,206
1973	335,558	328,259	83,242	245,017	7,299	2,515	4,784
1974	350,362	342,567	89,684	252,883	7,795	2,676	5,119
1975	367,053	359,034	95,166	263,868	8,019	2,784	5,235
1976	377,928	369,666	98,812	270,854	8,262	2,921	5,341
1977	388,531	379,869	101,685	278,184	8,662	3,130	5,532
1978	399,306	390,347	105,357	284,990	8,959	3,275	5,684
1979	408,415	399,339	110,587	288,752	9,076	3,374	5,702
1980	435,455	415,191	116,546	298,645	9,212	3,459	5,753
1981	462,463	431,647	126,364	305,283	9,224	3,532	5,692
1982	652,509	443,783	133,234	310,549	9,327	3,585	5,742
1983	664,039	452,881	136,496	316,385	9,637	3,700	5,937
1984	683,927	468,577	143,835	324,742	9,922	3,841	6,081
1985	754,928	475,663	146,918	328,745	4,952	1,761	3,191
1986	778,066	483,473	149,609	333,864	4,222	1,673	2,549
1987	815,179	489,772	152,096	337,676	3,632	1,467	2,165
1988	832,098	496,175	154,602	341,573	3,352	1,366	1,986
1989	1,041,853	515,387	162,311	353,076	3,155	1,278	1,877
1990	1,078,449	536,775	184,277	352,498	2,921	1,147	1,774
1991	1,103,236	549,615	187,277	362,338	2,747	1,124	1,623
1992	1,707,301	560,127	190,449	369,678	2,579	1,057	1,522
1993	1,759,843	572,122	193,234	378,888	2,409	979	1,430
1994	1,793,094	581,047	195,952	385,095	2,193	897	1,296

Note: RGEI stopped to accept the enrolling of new members from July 1985 onwards.

Source: Central Trust of China (1997), 'Statistical Data for Government Employees' Insurance', pp. 26-8, 101.

However, when looking closer, we find that between 1958 and 1979 the overall membership in all insurance schemes for this group of employees did not grow as much as from the early 1980s onwards. In the first 21 years, the number of insured covered by these schemes increased from 172,469 to 408,415, i.e. 4.19 percent on an average per year.

Table 7: Development of Membership of Insurance for Teaching and Administrative Staff of Private Schools (ITASPS) and Health Insurance for Government Employees' Dependents (HIGED), in persons

Year	ITASPS Insurance for Teaching and Administrative Staff of Private Schools			HIGED Health Insurance for Government Employees' Dependents		
	Total	Univ. & Jun. Coll.	Vocat., Sen. & Elem. School	Total	Central Gov't	Local Gov't
1980	11,052	480	10,572	-	-	-
1981	21,592	9,009	12,582	-	-	-
1982	23,369	10,110	13,259	176,030	54,325	121,705
1983	24,584	11,030	13,554	176,937	55,380	121,557
1984	25,673	11,618	14,055	179,573	57,709	121,864
1985	26,277	12,152	14,125	180,360	59,093	121,267
1986	26,974	12,900	14,074	180,739	60,240	120,499
1987	27,723	13,710	14,013	179,688	60,602	119,086
1988	28,110	14,285	13,825	176,749	60,442	116,307
1989	28,529	15,292	13,237	385,632	135,995	249,637
1990	31,213	16,947	14,266	390,239	143,735	246,504
1991	33,883	18,309	15,574	388,012	143,805	244,207
1992	36,075	19,352	16,723	950,307	336,933	613,374
1993	39,442	20,944	18,498	976,771	345,902	630,869
1994	42,864	22,727	20,137	982,642	346,152	636,490

Source: Central Trust of China (1997), 'Statistical Data for Government Employees' Insurance', pp. 26-8, 101.

From 1980 to 1988, the first year after the lift of martial law and the introduction of democracy in Taiwan, the coverage of social insurance schemes for employees of government institutions and private schools spurred from 435,455 to 832,098 with an annual increase rate of 8.43 percent. In the first years where democratic elections had been held, from

1989 to 1992, the government saw itself compelled to do more for these important occupational groups since they were vital for the maintenance of Kuomintang regime. Therefore, we can see in Table 5 that the coverage of these social insurance schemes jumped from 1,041,853 in 1989 to 1,707,301 in 1992; i.e. 63.87 percent growth within three years.

Whereas the development of the Government Employee Insurance (GEI) shows a steady increase in membership, the Retired Government Employee Insurance (RGEI) stopped accepting new members in the mid-1980s (see Table 6).

Table 8: Development of Health Insurance for Retired Government Employees (HIRGE), Health Insurance for Spouses of Retired Government Employees (HISRGE), in persons

	HIRGE Health Insurance for Retired Government Employees			HISRGE Health Insurance for Spouses of Retired Government Employees		
	Total	Central Gov't	Local Gov't	Total	Central Gov't	Local Gov't
1982	-	-	-	-	-	-
1983	-	-	-	-	-	-
1984	-	-	-	-	-	-
1985	41,406	10,409	30,997	26,087	6,668	19,419
1986	49,976	13,197	36,779	32,241	8,630	23,611
1987	68,080	16,546	51,534	45,649	11,305	34,344
1988	73,877	17,543	56,334	53,045	13,350	39,695
1989	62,332	14,920	47,412	45,973	11,713	34,260
1990	64,913	16,173	48,740	47,490	12,662	34,828
1991	68,041	17,625	50,416	49,331	13,554	35,777
1992	70,490	18,176	52,314	50,880	13,976	36,904
1993	74,085	1,897	55,188	53,389	14,629	38,760
1994	-	-	-	-	-	-

Source: Central Trust of China (1997), 'Statistical Data for Government Employees' Insurance', pp. 26-7.

The membership of the Insurance for Teaching and Administrative Staff of Private Schools (ITASPS), which was set up in 1980, reached only 42,964 in 1994. The increase in overall coverage of insurance schemes for employees of government institutions and private schools was brought, to a large extent, by the introduction of the Health Insurance for Government

Employees' Dependents (HIGED), which started with 176,030 members in 1982 and covered 982,642 dependents in the year 1994 (see Table 7). Here again, of course, we see the impact of the introduction of democracy on the construction of a more comprehensive social insurance system that not merely addressed the needs of key professionals, but also the common people, who now could, for the first time, check the power of the Kuomintang government by means of democratic elections.

Table 9: Development of Health Insurance for Retired Teaching and Administrative Staff of Private Schools (HIRTASPS), Health Insurance for Spouses of Retired Teaching and Administrative Staff of Private Schools (HISRTASPS), and Health Insurance for Dependents of Teaching and Administrative Staff of Private Schools (HIDTASPS), in persons

	HIRTASPS Health Insurance for Retired Teaching and Administrative Staff of Private Schools			HISRTASPS Health Insurance for Spouses of Retired Teaching and Administrative Staff of Private Schools			HIDTASPS Health Insurance for Dependents of Teaching and Administrative Staff of Private Schools		
	Central Gov't	Univ. & Junior Coll.	Vocat., Sen. & Elem. School	Central Gov't	Univ. & Junior Coll.	Vocat., Sen. & Elem. School	Central Gov't	Univ. & Junior Coll.	Vocat., Sen. & Elem. School
1984	182	101	81	-	-	-	-	-	-
1985	183	98	85	-	-	-	-	-	-
1986	310	174	136	131	79	52	-	-	-
1987	432	231	201	203	120	83	-	-	-
1988	550	277	273	240	137	103	-	-	-
1989	596	287	309	249	140	109	-	-	-
1990	664	325	339	280	164	116	3,954	2,314	1,640
1991	770	382	388	308	180	128	10,529	5,881	4,648
1992	821	429	392	332	197	135	35,690	18,881	16,809
1993	951	488	463	403	231	172	40,271	21,557	18,714
1994	-	-	-	-	-	-	44,038	23,833	20,205

Source: Central Trust of China (1997), 'Statistical Data for Government Employees' Insurance', pp. 28-9.

The Health Insurance for Retired Government Employees (HIRGE) catered to 74,085 persons, and the Health Insurance for Spouses of Retired

Government Employees (HISRGE) to 53,389 persons in the year 1993, the last year of their operation (see Table 8).

In an increasing effort to extend the number of social insurance programs for the privileged groups, the Kuomintang government set up the Health Insurance for Retired Teaching and Administrative Staff of Private Schools (HIRTASPS) in 1984, the Health Insurance for Spouses of Retired Teaching and Administrative Staff of Private Schools (HISRTASPS) in 1986, and the Health Insurance for Dependents of Teaching and Administrative Staff of Private Schools (HIDTASPS) in 1990 (Table 9).

The first two programs served more for increasing the government's legitimacy. The society at large could not benefit from them, since their membership never surpassed 1,000 members. But, the Health Insurance for Dependents of Teaching and Administrative Staff of Private Schools (HIDTASPS) managed to turn into a more sizeable scheme, incorporating 44,038 persons in the last year of its operation in 1994; thus, ending one year later than HIRGE, HISRGE, HIRTASPS, and HISRTASPS. The new program, the Health Insurance for Retired Employees and Their Dependents of Government Organizations and Private Schools (HIREDGOPS), lasted one year; it was comprised of the four programs just mentioned and covered 140,310 insured persons (see Table 10).

Table 10: Development of Health Insurance for Retired Employees and their Dependents of Government Organizations and Private Schools (HIREDGOPS), in persons

	All schemes for staff of government units and private schools	HIREDGOPS Health Insurance for Retired Employees and Their Dependents of Government Organizations and Private Schools (which operated only in 1994)				
		Total	Central Government	Local Government	University & Junior College	Vocat., Sen., Jun. High and Elem. School
1994	1,793,094	140,310	37,075	101,667	838	730

Source: Central Trust of China (1997), 'Statistical Data for Government Employees' Insurance', pp. 28-9.

Farmers' Health Insurance

In the last days of martial law rule, the Kuomintang decided to enhance its support among the crucial, forthcoming electorate of the masses of farmers.

In the beginning, however, it has only chosen to install an experimental program, i.e. the Temporary Provisions for Farmers' Health Insurance established in 1985. This program covered farmers who were heads of households (Ku, 1995: 82) and the number of insured was kept to a minimum. The Kuomintang tried to delay the increase of coverage of the program for as long as possible, as it was the case with the labor insurance program in the 1950s. In the first year of operation, 100,739 persons joined the scheme. One year later, only an additional 12,626 farmers joined the experimental program. With the fall of martial law, the membership almost doubled to 218,021 persons. During the subsequent year, membership even tripled, insuring 676,461 farmers.

In the year of general elections, 1989, this number doubled again, to 1,344,155, and continued to grow quickly until the year 1995, reaching a membership of 1,800,187 (see Table 11).

Table 11: The Development of Farmers' Health Insurance (1985-1996)

Year	No. of Persons Insured	Annual Increase in Membership in percent	Due Premium in million TWD	Total Benefits Paid in million TWD
Grand Total	*1,812,293*	-	*91,311*	*161,049*
1985	100,739	-	76	90
1986	113,365	12.53	479	911
1987	218,021	92.32	714	1,146
1988	676,461	310.27	2,319	2,385
1989	1,344,155	98.70	7,185	8,582
1990	1,571,296	16.90	12,290	18,212
1991	1,653,676	5.24	13,433	21,664
1992	1,695,167	2.50	13,891	27,395
1993	1,708,488	0.79	14,146	29,574
1994	1,737,740	1.71	14,280	32,941
1995	1,800,187	3.59	6,977	12,087
1996	1,812,293	0.67	5,514	6,057

Source: Bureau of Labor Insurance (1997), 'Yearbook of Labor Insurance Statistics', p. 300.

When looking at the benefits paid under this scheme we see a hefty increase until 1994, reaching 32,941 million TWD in 1994, causing a great extension of the welfare state system and especially a great involvement of the government in financing social welfare, which the KMT sought to avoid for a long time. But in the light of upcoming democratization, the KMT had no choice but to secure the support of the farming population, and to extend the benefits guaranteed by this scheme. While in 1989 premiums and benefits were not so far apart, the gap between granted benefits and contributions of the insured grew a great deal, with benefits amounting 230 percent of overall contributions in the year 1994.

In the year 1995, the overwhelming part of premiums and benefits were transferred to the National Health Insurance. Contributions for the Farmers' Health Insurance were divided 30 to 70, for the insured and the government respectively. The government's burden of financing this health insurance scheme was distributed as follows: 40 percent were raised by the central government, 20 percent by the provincial government, 10 percent by the city/county government, and the remaining 30 percent by municipalities (Chang, 1998: 36).

The National Health Insurance

Before the implementation of the universal National Health Insurance System, all major social insurance programs were sharply divided along occupational lines. The Labor Insurance, the Government Employee Insurance and Farmers' Health Insurance were the main columns of a rudimentary social insurance system that was modeled after the Bismarckian model of late 19th-century Germany. But with the coming of the National Health Insurance, and universal old-age allowances later on, the Taiwanese social security system turned into a mixed system, featuring both key characteristics of the Bismarckian and the Beveridgean social insurance tradition. Thus, the Taiwanese social insurance systemmust be regarded, by and large, as representing a mixed system after 1995, which is very similar to that of Italy and Spain (cf Aspalter, 2001c).

Articles 155 and 157 of the Constitution of the Republic of China respectively stipulate that the State 'shall establish a social insurance system in order to promote social welfare' and 'shall establish extensive services for sanitation and health protection and a system of public medical service in order to promote national health'. In 1992, in a special session of the National Assembly, an additional article, Additional Article 18(3), which was designated Additional Article 10(4) in the constitutional amendment of 1997, demanded that the 'State shall implement health insurance and promote the research and development of modern and traditional medicine' (BNHI, 1998). Whereas the former constitutional provisions were considered to be fulfilled by the implementation of the labor insurance system and the implementation of smaller health insurance systems for privileged societal groups, the new amendment of the year 1992 left no doubt that a new health insurance needed to be established.

When we trace back the planning period for a national health insurance system in Taiwan, it becomes clear that the end of marital law was responsible for the change in national health policy. In 1988, one year after the lifting of martial law, the powerful Council of Economic Planning and Development set up a task force, which began actively planning a national health insurance system. After the preliminary stage of planning was completed in June 1990, the Department of Health took over the subsequent planning work. In 1991 and 1993, a national health insurance planning task force within the Department of Health and the Bureau of National Health Insurance Preparatory Department were established respectively to lay the groundwork of the National Health Insurance program. On July 19, 1994, the parliament passed the National Health Insurance Act and the President promulgated it on August 2, the same year (cf BNHI, 1998; Chan and Xu, 1991; Hwang and Hill, 1997)

Interestingly, during the preparational period, the National Health Insurance was not a mandatory scheme from the very beginning; only after the October 3 amendment of 1994 it was turned into a compulsory health insurance scheme. After the Bureau of National Health Insurance Organizational Statute was passed on December 30, 1994, the Bureau of National Health Insurance was formally established on January 1, 1995. The National Health Insurance program took up operations on March 1, 1995. The two most important changes of the Taiwanese health system were the inclusion of virtually all of the population and the unification of previously existing health insurance schemes for privileged groups, such as employees of governmental organizations and private schools. At the end of 1997, the National Health Insurance program covered 20.49 million people, accounting for 96.29 percent of the population. The new unified health insurance, furthermore, reduced the variety of administrative bodies that were responsible for the formerly dispersed health insurance system. Before, health insurance programs spanned the purview of two branches of two different branches of government, the Executive Yuan and the Examination Yuan; three ministries/councils (the Ministry of Civil Service, Ministry of Interior, and the Council of Labor Affairs), and different insuring agencies (the Central Trust of China, The Labor Insurance Bureau of the Taiwan and Fujian Region). Therefore, it was hard to achieve consistency in premium rates, premium collection, benefits, and payment standards, and not all insured had the same protection (BNHI, 1998: cf also Hwang and Hill, 1997). However, the new uniform premium rate and payment system still prolongs the tradition of granting different premium rates to different occupational groups which has come to be the cornerstone of Taiwanese conservative social policy (Aspalter, 2001a).

The National Health Insurance Scheme program is organized into six different occupational groups. These six occupational groups, in addition, are divided into sub-brackets each featuring different contribution rates for employees, employers and the government.

Table 12: The Development of the National Health Insurance (1995-2095), in billion TWD

Year	Expected Premium Rate	Expected Premium Payments	Expected Expenditures	Expected Deficit
1995	6.07	161.2	173.8	12.6
2000	6.14	181.2	196.9	15.6
2005	6.30	200.9	219.8	18.9
2010	6.61	219.6	241.2	21.6
2015	7.05	237.8	262.0	24.3
2020	7.65	255.9	285.1	29.2
2025	8.44	276.6	310.9	34.2
2030	9.35	298.9	339.2	40.3
2035	10.13	316.4	362.8	46.4
2040	10.66	325.2	375.2	50.0
2045	10.95	323.9	376.2	52.4
2050	11.06	317.9	370.0	52.1
2055	11.10	312.3	362.1	49.8
2060	11.13	305.5	355.3	49.8
2065	11.08	296.4	345.2	48.8
2070	11.01	286.6	333.0	46.4
2075	11.07	279.5	325.1	45.6
2080	11.20	275.2	320.5	45.3
2085	11.24	269.4	313.7	44.3
2090	11.22	262.5	305.9	43.4
2095	11.17	254.4	296.5	42.1

Note: Calculations are based on an expected average birth rate of 1.805, the actual birth rate at the start of the new scheme.

Source: Tang Ching-li (1995), quoted in Zheng Kuan-chen (1995), 'Tai Wan Di Qu De Ren Kou Bian Qian Yu She Hui An Chuan', p. 109.

The first sub-bracket of the first main bracket includes public servants; persons employed by the government, and private school teachers. The employee comes up for 40 percent of contributions and the employer for the rest of 60 percent. In sub-bracket two, the contribution shares for private school teachers are, 40 percent for the employee, 30 for the employer and 30 for the State. In sub-bracket four of the main bracket one, self-employed persons have to pay 100 percent of the contributions by themselves. Industrial workers that are classified in main bracket two have to pay 60 percent by themselves. Their employers pay nothing and the State 40 percent. Farmers and fishermen of main bracket four have to pay 30 percent, the State sponsors 70 percent. For low-income people and military servicemen of main bracket five and six respectively, the state pays 100 percent. The highest premium rate has to be paid at an income of 48,001 TWD or more (approx. USD 1,560). Additional premium fees are collected for each dependent of the insured (Y.E. Chen, 1995).

Thus, the new redistributive effects of the new National Health Insurance are rather limited. The Taiwanese health insurance system is not a classical universal health insurance scheme. Whereas it is universal in terms of coverage and benefits, the contribution rate system still continues the tradition of preferential treatment for politically important occupational groups, such as the military and government employees. The preferential treatment of the group of farmers and low-income persons in comparison to the rest of the population is a new feature of the Taiwanese health insurance system, which reflects the new development of politics in general, and social policy in particular, in the decade preceding the implementation of the National Health Insurance program.

Table 12 displays the expected future development of average premium rates for the National Health Insurance, expecting a premium rate of about 11 percent around the year 2050. Deficits are expected not to exceed 52.4 million TWD in the mid-2040s, declining thereafter.

Health Insurance Scheme for Delegates and Elected Officers of Local Government

The Kuomintang government replied to new pressures stemming from new party competition in democratic elections moreover with the introduction of a health insurance scheme for delegates and elected officers of local governments who formerly received no preferential treatment in social policy. These officers became now even more vital in winning elections. They influence a great deal the people in their election districts, most of whom they know personally, and most of whom they in their decision-making. Due to the Single Non-transferable Vote System applied in Taiwan, also a proper distribution is needed between the votes of candidates of the same party within each election district (when there are more than one, as it is usually the case). A failure to do so results in a possible loss of a parliamentary seat; and these delegates and elected officers help a great deal to ensure an even distribution of votes among different candidates of the KMT.

The delegates and elected officers of local governments come around the houses; shout up into the houses from the streets, they give speeches on cars running slowly through the neighborhoods. Potential non-voters are looked after especially, and the sick and the very old who cannot go to the ballot box by themselves are brought there by voluntary helpers organized by these local government officers. Success in gaining or maintain local government control was and still is a highly rewarding job, since the richest political party of the world, the Kuomintang, pays a great deal of money to its local representatives who help the KMT to secure as much as possible its grip on power at local government level.

Table 13 shows that the new Health Insurance Scheme for Delegates and Elected Officers of Local Government was one of the most important new social policies in the early democratic era. The membership of this scheme was stable at around 28,000 insured persons between 1989 and 1992. However, most benefits that were granted under this scheme were in-kind benefits, and not cash benefits. This went along with conservative concepts of social policy applied in Taiwan (and elsewhere in East Asia, cf Aspalter, 2001a) that sought to minimize cash transfers to welfare recipients.

Table 13: The Development of the Health Insurance Scheme for Delegates and Elected Officers of Local Government During the Time of First Democratic Elections (1989-1992)

	No. of Insured		Total		Cash Benefit Payments		Medical Benefit Payments
	persons	cases	mill. TWD	cases	mill. TWD	cases	mill. TWD
1989	28,507	4,886	2.8	39	1.9	4,847	0.8
1990	27,416	258,770	230.8	625	31.1	258,145	199.7
1991	28,361	335,679	291.1	627	33.5	335,052	257.5
1992	28,343	671,620	554.8	801	49.3	670,819	505.4

Source: calculated from Department of Statistics, Ministry of Interior (1993), 'Interior Statistics Monthly', pp. 36-7.

Unemployment Insurance Benefits of the Labor Insurance

The West often belittles or ignores the negative consequences of globalization that East Asian economies have experienced. However, the flight of labor-intensive industries to cheaper production sites outside Taiwan, such as Mainland China, Vietnam, Thailand and Malaysia, led to severe structural changes of the economy. These changes manifest in structural unemployment, which is not short-term, but long-term in nature. The labor market, and especially also the education system, responds only very slowly to changes in the global and local economy. Taiwan needed to upgrade its production, from labor-intensive to highly capital-intensive production lines in order to continue to play a vital role in the international economy (cf Aspalter, 2001d). Companies relocated factories to Mainland China and, consequently, many lower skilled laborers lost their jobs in Taiwan.

The government did not previously address the issue of unemployment, but with increasing numbers of jobless young as well as elder people, the concerns over the problem of long-term unemployment rose. To rely only on official unemployment rates means to overlook the problem of unemployment of the elder workforce, i.e. those between 50 and 65 years of age, and that of women. Women and aged workers do not regard themselves as unemployed because they do not expect unemployment benefits (since today most of them are not entitled to such benefits).

Table 14: Unemployment Rate per Age Group in 1997

Age class	Total	Male Unemployment Rate	Female Unemployment Rate
15-19	**7,35**	**6,52**	**8,25**
20-24	**6,76**	**7,46**	**6,23**
25-29	**3,68**	**4,11**	**3,09**
30-34	2,15	2,64	1,34
35-39	1,84	2,33	1,05
40-44	1,63	2,08	0,89
45-49	1,61	2,1	0,73
50-54	1,76	2,34	0,53
55-59	1,31	1,71	0,31
60-64	0,8	1,01	1,21
65 + over	0,28	0,32	0,12
Total	2,72	2,94	2,37
15-65	0,0270	0,030	0,0235

Source: Directorate-General of Budget, Accounting and Statistics (1997a), 'Yearbook of Manpower Survey Statistics', pp. 139-41.

Therefore it is important to note the fall in the category of people not in the workforce, but who are in fact unemployed. Young people, as well, may think about studying at university due to the absence of realistic job opportunities and, thus, join the workforce much later than they could otherwise. This phenomenon is called hidden unemployment. Only when looking at both, unemployment figures and the figures of persons not participating in the workforce, one can catch a realistic picture of the unemployment problem (see Tables 14 to 16).

Only people who looked actively for employment in the last couple of weeks are referred to as being out of employment. Two years mandatory military service in Taiwan leads to a lesser degree of youth unemployment among the male population. Unemployment rates in the year 1997 for girls aged 15 to 19 were as high as 8.25 percent; for boys they were 6.52 percent. In the group of young men aged 20 to 24, unemployment exceeds that of young women in the same age group, i.e. 7,46 compared to 6.23 percent respectively (Table 14).

When looking at the percentages of elder men and women over 50 and comparing them to the percentages for men and women in the age group of 45 to 49 years old, we see that forced unemployment amounts to 35 percent and more for both genders (Table 16).

Table 15: The Problem of Hidden Unemployment: High Number of Persons not Participating in the Labor Force in 1997, in thousand persons

Age Group	Male	Female
15-19	792	803
20-24	241	357
25-29	67	295
30-34	34	374
35-39	35	367
40-44	33	338
45-49	38	308
50-54	48	243
55-59	85	291
60-64	144	282
65 + over	814	751

Source: Directorate-General of Budget, Accounting and Statistics (1997a), 'Yearbook of Manpower Survey Statistics', pp. 151.

A comparison with earlier governmental statistics shows, however, that forced unemployment due to aging has decreased in the previous decade. The unemployment rates for those between 60 and 64 years of age were 48.1 percent for men and 84.7 percent for women (cf Tsai, 1989: 85).

Since the size of the unemployed population grew and the fact that the government needed to ease social unrest, and to avoid it as much as possible, due to the looming military intervention by Mainland China, the Kuomintang finally installed an unemployment benefit system in 1998.

Table 16: Percentage of Persons not Participating in the Labor Force in Overall Civilian Population Aged 15 Years and Over in 1997

Age Group	Male	Female
15-19	**81.31**	**82.86**
20-24	**37.53**	**40.15**
25-29	**7.51**	**32.85**
30-34	3.53	39.57
35-39	3.71	39.50
40-44	3.84	40.00
45-49	*5.64*	*46.73*
50-54	**11.48**	**58.41**
55-59	**20.68**	**69.12**
60-64	**40.56**	**79.21**
65 + over	**87.15**	**96.15**
Total	**28.91**	**54.35**

Source: Calculated from the data in Directorate-General of Budget, Accounting and Statistics (1997a), 'Yearbook of Manpower Survey Statistics', pp. 151.

The then Chairman of the Council of Labor Affairs, Chan Hou-sheng, and the then Prime Minister, Hsiao Wan-chang, were the leading political figures behind the introduction of the new unemployment insurance benefit scheme which had been subordinated to the Labor Insurance. The introduction of the new scheme was expected to face great difficulties since the majority of both leading parties, the Kuomintang and the Democratic Progressive Party, did not support unemployment insurance due to their conservative social policy stands (cf TAO, 1997).

Under the new scheme, benefits of 50 percent of the insured's last income are paid to up to three, six, or eight months when the insured gets unemployed for the first time, thereafter he or she may use up the rest of a maximum of six, twelve, or sixteen months; the length of these maximums depends on the time the unemployed was insured up to then (cf CLA, 1999). With over ten years of insurance, the insured can apply for the maximum of benefits, that is 8 months for the first time of unemployment and 16 months all together (see Table 17).

Table 17: Different Periods for Payment of Unemployment Benefits

Condition	Every time	All together
Less than five years of contribution	3 months	6 months
Five to ten years of contribution	6 months	12 months
More than ten years of contribution	8 months	16 months

Source: Bureau of Labor Insurance (1999), 'Lao Gong Bao Xuan She Ye Gei Fu Shen Jing Zhen Zhi', p. 2.

Social Assistance and Social Services

In the development of the welfare state system in Taiwan, social assistance did not play a major part until very recently. The first piece of legislation regarding social assistance was the Social Relief Law in 1943, enacted still in Mainland China. This law was designed to offer help to segments of society according to their particular circumstances, but not according to their financial situation. Aid was recommended to those only who were poor because of high age, youth, pregnancy, disability or disaster (cf Ku, 2002).

For almost the next four decades nothing changed in this matter. Poverty was perceived to be self-made, and the individual had the responsibility for not getting poor and for dealing with this problem. Therefore, the government paid little attention to the problem of poverty in the 1950s and 1960s. In the early 1970s, the Taiwan Provincial government and the Taipei city government implemented two new community development programs that were influenced by the War on Poverty in the United States a decade earlier. These programs were the Shao-Kang program ('little well-off') implemented in Taiwan Province and the An-Kang program ('healthy and wealthy') set up in Taipei city. Both new schemes aimed at eradicating poverty by launching a wave of new social assistance benefits and social services, including vocational training, short-term loans for the unemployment, residential care for family-less chronically ill and disabled children, social assistance benefits and low-cost housing at the community level for low-income families (H.S. Chan, 1985: 327-8). Before 1980, only the local and provincial governments were in charge of providing social assistance, but not the central government (Ku, 1995: 38).

In the year 1980, the government changed its attitude in the field of social assistance to the poor and implemented the new Social Assistance Law of 1980. It started to determine the need for social assistance by focusing on the financial means of the poor and not the causes of their poverty. The Social Assistance Law of 1980, however, abstained from giving a clear formula for determining the deserving poor. Hence, government officials could and did set up an incredibly low poverty line, to limit the use of government funds needed for social assistance programs.

Only the new Social Assistance Law of 1997 introduced a poverty line, which was set at 60 percent of per capita consumption expenditures in the previous year. Some scholars suggest that up to 5 percent of the population may now qualify for social assistance with this new poverty line (Ku, 1995, 2002; MOI, 1998a).

The number of poor people receiving indoor relief was constantly increasing from 2,571 people in 1950 to 11,334 people in 1990. Conversely, the number of people receiving outdoor relief began to decline rapidly in the 1970s. As a result the number of recipients of out-door relief was reduced by more than 85 percent in the same period (see Table 18).

Table 18: Poor People Receiving Benefits of the Social Assistance Scheme (1950-1990)

Year	Indoor relief	As % of population	Outdoor relief	As % of population
1950	2,571	0.03	736,054	10.10
1955	4,091	0.05	731,709	8.06
1960	6,606	0.06	1,370,532	12.07
1965	7,030	0.06	1,153,080	9.73
1970	8,415	0.06	466,676	3.18
1975	7,764	0.05	122,916	0.76
1980	9,522	0.05	115,666	0.65
1985	10,622	0.06	113,692	0.59
1990	11,334	0.06	107,312	0.53

Source: Andy Yin-han Kuo (2000), 'The Development of Social Assistance as an Issue of Central-local Relations in Taiwan', p. 10.

In the year 1986, a total number of 114,076 persons – which counted for 0.58 percent of the population – received low-income assistance benefits. The administration of low-income assistance was separated between the Taiwan Provincial government, the Taipei city government and the Kaohsiung city government, each running its own program. In the 1990s, the importance of social assistance grew, however, still lagged far behind that of social insurance. In 1994, the government started the Living Allowance for Middle-Low Income Elderly People. In the year 1999, there were 185,000 persons; out of which 19,575 persons were regarded being low-income earners, and 172,277 middle-income earners (MOI, 1993: 11-1; MOI, 1998a: 44-5). In the field of low-income earners, the number of the poorest of the poor had been reducing in the 1990s (see Tables 19-21). However, the absolute number of poor old people was increasing at the same time, e.g. from 1985 to 1995 by 71.7 percent. The relative share of poor households headed by an elderly person among all households headed by the elderly has been decreasing from 12.4 to 7.2 percent respectively (cf Y.Z. Chan, 1997: 21).

After having proved to be a considerable contestant in the first national elections challenging the long-term ruling Kuomintang for the first time, the Democratic Progressive Party began to concentrate on the issue of social welfare, i.e. old-age allowances, in order to win elections in 1993. The representatives of the Democratic Progressive Party put forward for the first time in Taiwanese history a universal social assistance benefit for all citizens amounting to up to 5,000 TWD. After these elections, in all counties, in which the DPP won, old-age allowances had been introduced; however, some of these schemes could not be paid out since representatives of the Kuomintang and the New Party often blocked the financial support of this new scheme in county and city councils (obviously to hamper the otherwise guaranteed success of popular DDP social policies). In 1997, the issue again raised and significantly changed overall election outcomes, catapulting the DPP into the first place, and this also in terms of absolute number of votes. In the second part of this book, the author deals in detail with the 1997 and 1998 elections and the impact of the issue of social assistance benefits for the elderly.

In the light of the nearing first free presidential election in Taiwan in March 1996, President Lee Teng-hui also introduced a universal old-age farmers' allowance. Though the government tried to explain the introduction of the new scheme with its wish 'to take care of old-age farmers livelihood and promote farmers' benefits' (BLI, 1997: 342), most Taiwanese understood the timing of the new act and the reasons for the long period of time that passed by, i.e. four and a half decades, before the Kuomintang implemented the first significant, large-scale social assistance scheme in Taiwanese history. The cause of implementing this new scheme was given by the upcoming presidential election in March 1996.

On June 8, 1995, the Council of Agriculture of the central government promulgated the new Old-age Farmers' Allowance Act. The operation of the allowance scheme was authorized to the Bureau of Labor Insurance, and first applications were accepted from mid-August 1995 onwards. Those farmers who were over 65 years of age and who participated in the Farmers' Health Insurance for more than 6 months could obtain the TWD 3,000 high old-age farmers' allowance. This new allowance is granted to farmers' until they pass away. In the Taiwan provincial area, the central government bore 70 percent of the costs, and the provincial government 30 percent. In Taipei and Kaohsiung municipal areas, the load of financing the farmers' old-age allowance was divided equally between the city governments and the central government (BLI, 1997). In the year 1999, 703,000 old farmers received the old-age farmers' allowance (see Table 19).

Table 19: Elderly Receiving Income Support Assistance and Old Farmer Allowance (1994-1999)

Year	Number of Elderly Receiver	Number of Old Farmer Receiver	Number of Total Receiver	As % of total elderly (over 65 years old)
1994	88,282		88,282	5.65
1995	301,016	331,478	632,494	38.78
1996	272,878	366,011	638,889	37.77
1997	157,075	427,222	584,297	33.35
1998	192,000	442,000	634,000	not available
1999	185,000	703,000	888,000	not available

Source: Andy Yin-han Kuo (2000), 'The Development of Social Assistance as an Issue of Central-local Relations in Taiwan', p. 15.

Table 20: The Number of Low-Income Households (1988-1998)

Year	Total	Class 1 (highest degree of poverty)	Class 2 (medium high degree of poverty)	Class 3 (less high degree of poverty)
1988	39,355	11,548	14,153	13,654
1989	37,129	11,119	13,184	12,826
1990	40,994	12,013	14,968	14,013
1991	42,665	12,012	14,818	15,835
1992	43,780	12,216	14,598	16,966
1993	46,717	12,005	15,298	19,414
1994	48,182	9,983	16,114	22,085
1995	48,580	8,755	17,160	22,665
1996	49,307	7,855	17,884	23,568
1997	49,780	6,544	18,486	24,750
1998	54,977	5.797	20,702	28,478

Source: Department of Statistics, Ministry of Interior (1998a), 'Monthly Bulletin of Interior Statistics', pp. 38-9.

Other major social assistance schemes in Taiwan are the living assistance for low-income families, the old-age allowances on county and city level, the income support for the elderly within low-income families, the old farmer allowance, and social assistance for calamities and emergencies, such as typhoons, floods, fires, and earthquakes. With the exception of old-age allowances for senior citizens, which were introduced by the Democratic Progressive Party, all other social assistance benefits had been means-tested before 1999. In that year, the Kuomintang government, which apparently could not justify the means testing of Old-age Farmer Allowance, transformed the scheme into a non-means-tested one.

Table 21: The Number of Low-Income Persons (1988-1997)

Year	Total	Class 1 (highest degree of poverty)	Class 2 (medium high degree of poverty)	Class 3 (less high degree of poverty)
1988	111,477	14,603	45,272	51,602
1989	100,495	13,867	39,872	46,756
1990	114,220	15,376	48,916	49,928
1991	116,225	15,326	48,089	52,810
1992	115,284	15,729	46,890	52,665
1993	118,502	15,373	46,436	56,693
1994	115,748	12,336	44,204	59,208
1995	114,707	10,794	42,824	61,089
1996	115,542	9,533	42,738	63,271
1997	116,056	7,906	42,852	65,298
1997	125,433	6,769	45,664	73,000

Source: Department of Statistics, Ministry of Interior (1998a), 'Monthly Bulletin of Interior Statistics', pp. 38-9.

Once again the Kuomintang jumped on the bandwagon of progressive social policy proposals of the DPP, which successfully advanced universal old-age allowances before.

The funding of these major social assistance schemes varies a great deal. Whereas living assistance and old-age allowances for senior citizens are funded on city and county government level, the old farmer allowance is fully sustained by resources of the central government. The Income Support for the Elderly in Low-Income Families, in contrast, is financed partly by central, provincial and county/city governments (see Table 22).

The reasons for the differences in financing the schemes are to be found in the political circumstances at the time these schemes had been implemented. In general, the KMT tried to keep social spending to a minimum by fully delegating major welfare responsibilities to local and provincial government level; the major example for this is the Living Assistance for Low-Income Families. The DPP, originally, had a tripartite system of financing welfare programs in mind. But with the majority of parliamentary seats held by the KMT, the DPP was compelled to set up their own welfare programs, funded fully by county or city governments. The major case example for this is old-age allowance for senior citizens. The Old-age Farmer Allowance was to ensure the KMT's support by the countryside in the upcoming 1996 presidential election. To guarantee the nationwide support of the farming population for Lee Teng-hui, the universal Old Farmer Allowance (since many county/city governments were not controlled by the KMT anymore) had to be installed on central government level. Sometimes compromises are possible, depending on the political discourse of the day when the new schemes are set up, an example for this is the Income Support for the Elderly within Low-Income Families, which features a tripartite structure of funding.

Table 22: Eligibility and Funding of Social Assistance Schemes

Benefit	Eligibility	Funding provided by
Living Assistance for Low-Income Families (from 1980 onwards)	Means-tested benefit	1. Taipei and Kaohsiung City: 100 % funded by city government 2. Other counties
The Old-Age Allowance on county and city level (from 1993 onwards)	DPP ruled counties and cities (the vast majority): Universal benefit KMT ruled counties and cities: Not applicable	DPP ruled counties and cities: 100 % funded by county and city governments KMT ruled counties and cities: Not applicable
Income Support for the Elderly within Low-Income Families (from 1994 onwards)	Means-tested benefit	before 1999: 1. Central government: 50 % 2. Provincial government: 25 % 3. County/city government: 25%
The Old Farmer Allowance (from 1995 onwards)	Before 1999: Means-tested benefit After 1999: Universal benefit	100% funded by the central government

Source: adapted from Andy Yin-han Kuo (2000), 'The Development of Social Assistance as an Issue of Central-local Relations in Taiwan', p. 15.

Today, social assistance has come to play a vital role in the Taiwanese welfare system. A look back into the year 1986 shows that social assistance occupied already 8.36 percent of welfare state expenses, and this was before the introduction of major social assistance schemes of the 1990s. Welfare services, which counted for 27.85 percent of welfare state benefits, forms a major column of the Taiwanese welfare state. The weight of social services in overall welfare provision is outstanding when compared to e.g. that of Japan, the United States and the United Kingdom (Table 23).

In November 1940, the Kuomintang government in Mainland China formally established a Ministry of Social Affairs, but after the retreat to Taiwan, it was dissolved, and the functions of providing social assistance and social welfare services were transferred to the Ministry of Interior. The provision of personal social services, especially in the field of family counseling, youth guidance and institutional care, had been, for the most part, relying on voluntary and charitable agencies.

Table 23: The Distribution of Social Assistance, Social Services, Medical Care and Social Insurance in 1986: A Four-Country Comparison

	Taiwan	Japan	USA	UK
Social Assistance	8.36	3.73	17.77	24.60
Social Services	27.85	6.30	7.28	5.70
Medical Care	33.60	16.02	7.64	27.30
Social Insurance	30.19	73.93	67.93	42.40
Total	100.00	100.00	100.00	100.00

Source: Tsai Song-zhao (1990), 'She Hui Fu Li Zheng Ce – Fu Li Yu Jing Ji De Zeng He', p. 231.

In the 1960s, a range of social welfare services had been introduced after the implementation of the government's Current Social Policies of the Principle of Livelihood. Therein, the Kuomintang government proposed the advancement of employment services, public housing, and welfare services for disadvantaged groups of the population, social education and community development. In the 1970s, the government intended to cooperate more closely with welfare NGOs in the provision of welfare services (cf Bai, 1979: 495), but social welfare organizations only prospered in the 1980s and were promoted by the opposition movement and not the government. In the postwar era, governmental welfare services had been directed mostly toward servicemen, government employees and veterans. Hence, the proportion of welfare funds and services going to disadvantaged groups, such as low-income households, blue-collar laborers, farmers, senior citizens, children, and the disabled, has been rather limited (cf Chan and Yang, 2001; Ku, 1995; H.S. Chan, 1985).

The Child Welfare Law of 1973 was the first welfare law that particularly focused on disadvantaged persons, but the Kuomintang continued to insist on its policy that families and parents should bear primary responsibility for child care and that the state should only intervene in emergencies such as family breakdown, child abuse and so on (Ku,

1955: 39). Before the 1970s, social services had been provided on a piecemeal basis. Only after social unrest and a series of disturbances cropped up between 1976 and 1979, which shed light on the insufficient supply of social services and social assistance, the government began to draft laws for needy groups. Subsequently, the Kuomintang set up three new laws in 1980: the Social Assistance Law, the Senior Citizens' Welfare Law, and the Welfare Law for the Disabled and Handicapped (see App. 5).

The Social Assistance Law of 1980 required that the provincial government and the two municipal cities of Taipei and Kaohsiung were responsible for the provision of personal social services, such as family assistance, medical treatment, emergency assistance and disaster aid. The other two new social laws of 1980 demanded that the social welfare sections of county/city governments should bear all responsibilities of caring for the elderly (aged 70 and over) and for disabled and handicapped persons respectively. The new regulations required the set up of residential care and other personal social services; either directly provided by the government or indirectly by voluntary and private organizations that were supported by governmental authorities (H.S. Chan, 1985: 328-34). In 1989, the government enacted the Youth Welfare Law. The Women's Welfare Law and the Social Workers Law followed in the early 1990s.

Table 24: Expenditure on Social Services by Groups of Recipient, (1991-1997), in billion TWD and percent

Year	*Amount, in billion TWD*	*Handi-capped*	*Elderly*	*Children*	*Women*	*Community Develop-ment*	*Others*
1991	4,701	27.23	26.88	21.61	0.75	1.07	22.46
1992	5,624	57.92	18.88	12.95	1.38	1.42	7.45
1993	6,279	55.38	25.97	7.62	1.67	2.07	7.29
1994	7,337	51.29	26.77	11.28	1.87	2.04	6.74
1995	7,908	50.05	25.99	12.59	1.96	2.40	7.00
1996	7,444	50.37	24.40	12.02	2.59	2.55	8.07
1997	7,353	52.27	22.23	11.28	2.51	2.54	9.17

Source: 'White Paper on Social Welfare', quoted in Ku Yeun-wen (2002), 'Towards a Taiwanese Welfare State? Demographic Change, Politics and Social Policy'.

The Future Challenge of Providing Social Welfare for the Elderly

All East Asian welfare state systems is increasingly challenged by a rapidly aging population. Japan is heading this development, and the percentage of elderly over 60 years of age in Japan will reach 20 percent around the year 2025 (HSU, 1989: 96). In Taiwan in the year 2025, there will be around 17 percent of the population that are older than 65. Ten years later, it will be more than 21 percent (see Table 25). The old age dependency ratios will increase more than threefold, from 0.11 in the year 1995 to 0.35 in 2035. A decline in youth dependency ratios, from 0.35 to 0.27 in the same period, cannot set off or diminish the consequences of an aging society. The working-aged population, between 15 and 65, will have to sustain a much greater number of people who will heavily rely on them for welfare and care provision. The increased number of elderly extends overproportionally the burden of the dependent's family, since medical expenditures increase progressively during old age.

Table 25: Expected Demographic Changes and Increasing Dependency Ratios Caused by the Fast Aging Society (1995-2035)

	Total Population in thousand	Group of 0-14 years old (A)	Group of 15-64 years old (B)	Group of 64 and over years old and over (C)	Old Age Dependency ratio (C/B)	Total Dependency ratio ((A+C)/B)
1995	21,256	24.09	68.44	7.48	0.11	0.46
2000	22,200	21.82	69.73	8.45	0.12	0.43
2005	23,108	20.68	69.98	9.34	0.13	0.43
2010	23,956	20.20	69.78	10.02	0.14	0.43
2015	24,670	19.51	69.06	11.43	0.17	0.45
2020	25,183	18.55	67.37	14.08	0.21	0.48
2025	25,535	17.58	65.42	17.01	0.26	0.53
2030	25,750	17.04	63.32	19.64	0.31	0.58
2035	25,799	17.09	61.57	21.34	0.35	0.62

Source: Chen Wu-hsiung (1996), 'Wo Guo Lao Ren Fu Li Zheng Ce De Xian Xing Zuo Fang Yu Wei Lai Chan Wang', p. 6.

The government of Taiwan needs to take this development more into account and prepare the welfare state system for the future wave of challenges in order to accommodate the growing need of the elderly population. Furthermore, the declining of average family size adds to the troubles of the elderly people who, then, often find themselves increasingly abandoned or not taken care of sufficiently. In 1981, the average household size in Taiwan was 4.7 persons; 16 years later, in 1997, the average size of household has been reduced to 3.5 persons (see Table 26). When looking at the statistics regarding the size of low-income households, we can easily make out the reasons for poverty, i.e. living on one's own. Of course, most poor people living alone are elderly people either living apart from their children – for the most part, due to migration or their wish to form a nuclear family; but also due to changed personal attitudes. Less and less younger people are willing to support their elderly family members (cf L.Z. Xu, 1989: 143). Nowadays, there are also many elderly couples become social assistance recipients.

Table 26: The Size of Low-Income Households (1988-1997)

	All Classes	Class 1 (highest degree of poverty)	Class 2 (medium high degree of poverty)	Class 3 (less high degree of poverty)
1988	2.83	1.26	3.19	3.77
1989	2.70	1.24	3.02	3.64
1990	2.78	1.27	3.26	3.56
1991	2.72	1.27	3.24	3.33
1992	2.63	1.28	3.21	3.10
1993	2.53	1.28	3.03	2.92
1994	2.40	1.23	2.74	2.69
1995	2.36	1.23	2.49	2.68
1996	2.34	1.21	2.38	2.68
1997	2.33	1.20	2.31	2.63
1998	2.28	1.16	2.20	2.56

Source: calculated from Department of Statistics, Ministry of Interior (1998a), ' Monthly Bulletin of Interior Statistics', pp. 38-9.

Modernization, thus, implies inevitably a long-term extension of welfare needs of the elderly population. In Taiwan, regional differences in the extension of welfare needs are caused by different shares of elderly population and the differences in family welfare provision between the countryside and the cities. The large cities, such as Taipei, Kaohsiung, and Taichung, attract a great number of young people who seek employment there or who stay in these large cities after they finish e.g. their tertiary education. A new phenomenon is welfare tourism, i.e. elderly people coming, especially, to Taipei in order to profit from better welfare benefits and services of this pioneer city in the field of social welfare (CHC, 1997).

It are rural, rather remote, and less populated areas of Taiwan in which the relative share of elderly people that are receiving low-income allowances is the highest, namely Nantou county, Chiayi county, Penghu country, Kaohsiung county,[17] Miaoli county and Hualien county.

Nonetheless, the majority of elderly people receiving income maintenance support in form of low-income allowances are living in highly populated cities and counties, such as Taipei city, Taipei county, Taoyuan county, Changhua county, Taichung county, Kaohsiung county and Kaohsiung city (see Table 27).

Table 27: Selective Indicators of Welfare Need and Welfare Provision for the Elderly at the End of the 1990s

County/City	Elderly Population in 1996 (aged 65 and over)	Elderly Recipients of Low-Income Allowance	Elderly Recipients of Low-Income Allowance, % of Elderly Population	Registered Elderly Population Living Alone, in 1999	Illegal Homes for the Elderly, in 1998	Percentage of Poor Population
Taipei city	222,234	45,871	20,6	not available	187	0.65
Taipei county	194,519	14,307	7.3	2,560	107	0.35
Taichung city	51,481	4,993	9.7	1,072	40	0.16
Tainan city	47,928	3,458	7.2	773	40	0.36
Tainan county	99,833	15,366	15.3	4,359	40	0.42
Taoyuan county	110,352	20,884	18,9	1,970	40	0.46
Kaohsiung county	89,641	31,319	34.9	3,093	40	0.46
Taichung county	89,969	18,235	20.2	2,208	36	0.23
Keelung city	29,281	4,751	16.2	1,332	27	0.39
Changhua county	102,196	6,707	6.5	2,027	27	0.49
Pingtung county	76,965	23,038	29.9	2,883	25	1.15
Kaohsiung city	84,135	20,805	24.7	not available	22	0.84
Chiayi county	57,921	22,336	38.5	1,475	17	0.66
Ilan county	40,297	2,710	6.7	909	17	0.83
Hsinchu city	27,982	1,966	7.0	597	13	0.19
Nantou county	48,477	19,175	39.5	2,426	13	0.86
Chiayi city	19,971	2,583	12.9	626	12	0.55
Hualien county	35,340	11,673	33.0	2,201	11	1.34
Hsinchu county	35,682	904	2.5	817	4	0.30
Miaoli county	52,122	17,331	33.2	1,101	4	0.51
Yunlin county	72,249	17,913	24.7	2,163	4	0.82
Taitung county	25,869	6,309	24.3	2,469	3	2.53
Penghu county	11,061	3,958	35.7	805	-	2.83

Sources: Chen Wu-Hsiung (1996), 'Wo Guo Lao Ren Fu Li Zheng Ce: Xian Xing Cuo Shi Yu She Lai Zhan Wang', p. 11; Huang Song-lin (2000), 'Domiciliary Care for the Elderly People Living Alone in Taiwan Province', p. 5; updated internal document of the Social Welfare Department, MOI (1998b), 'Ben Shen She Li An Lao Ren An, Liao Yang Ji Gou Yi Lan Biao'; and Department of Statistics, MOI (1998a), 'Monthly Bulletin of Interior Statistics', pp. 38-9.

The official numbers for registered elderly people living alone do not lead to any concrete conclusion, except for the fact that the registration of elderly people residing alone varies a great deal between counties and cities. The number of illegal homes (not or not yet registered) for the elderly is alarming, since they offer mostly sub-standard living facilities and care services; and this highly overpriced (EXP, 1998). Taipei city and county are again leader in this development; showing first, that homes for the elderly here are more lucrative and, second, that people in this region can afford these homes (Table 27). But the need for governmental social welfare is highly connected to the number of elderly people and the degree of poverty in each county and city. Thus, in Taipei city, Taipei county, Taoyuan county and Changhua county, the need for social welfare services for the elderly is the highest when comparing different counties and cities with each other.

Table 28: The Development of Nationwide Social Organizations in the First Years of Democratization, in absolute numbers (1986-1991)

Year	Total	Medical Organizations	Social Service Organizations	Others
1989	952	114	115	723
1990	1,007	114	114	779
1991	1,388	220	201	967
1992	1,536	155	227	1154

Source: calculated from Department of Statistics, Ministry of Interior (1993), 'Interior Statistics Monthly', pp. 38-9.

Table 29: Social Relief Organizations for the Aged in the First Years of Democratization (1986-1991)

Year	Houses	Inmates
1986	37	10,483
1987	35	10,537
1988	38	10,873
1989	40	10,474
1990	43	10,756
1991	45	10,707

Source: calculated from Department of Statistics, Ministry of Interior (1993), 'Interior Statistics Monthly', p. 30.

Apart from profit-seeking companies that provide housing and social services to the increasingly elderly population, there are also a growing number of social service organizations. But, an overall increase in the number of social service organizations, from 115 to 227 in 1989 and 1992 respectively, did not result in a significant improvement for the elderly since the number of inmates in houses provided by social relief organizations did not increase accordingly, but rather did not undergo any significant change at all (see Tables 28 and 29).

Since the proclamation of the Democratic Progressive Party's intention of establishing a welfare state during the 1993 County Commissioner and City Major Elections (cf Hwang and Hill: 92), major columns of a Taiwanese welfare state system had been constructed, especially with regard to national health insurance, extended social assistance and social services, and unemployment insurance. But, hitherto the question of pensions has not been solved. The initial attempts of DPP county commissioners and city mayors of granting social assistance to all elderly people regardless of their income meant, in fact, that it tried to establish a universal, non-contributionary pension system along the British/Swedish model. Indeed, many parliamentarians and government administrators of the DPP visited countries in Europe, and especially Sweden, and studied their welfare state institutions (CHC, 1997; LWI, 1998).

The new old-age allowance schemes first introduced by the Tainan county candidate of the DPP in the 1993 County Commissioner and City Mayor Elections (cf Kwon, 1998), and then by all other DPP candidates, were intended to help the elderly especially in the period before the national pension scheme is implemented.

The first stage of planning for the national pension system began in March 1994, and by May 1995 a preliminary report was completed (L. Chan, 1994; H.H. Chen, 2000). During the main phase of the election campaign for the County Commissioner and City Mayor Elections of 1997, the Council for Economic Planning and Development of the central government proposed the establishment of a country-wide pension program by the year 2000, and the detailed plan for its implementation should be finalized by June 1998.

The CEPD stated that the national pension program should be compulsory for soldiers, public officials, teachers, other laborers, and citizens over 25 years who are not insured elsewhere. After 40 years of contributing to the pension system, a monthly pension of about TWD 7,000 to 8,500[18] will be paid to the elderly. The envisaged monthly contribution is put at TWD 912, of which the government will sponsor 20 percent. The remainder will have to be shared by employers and employees. The portion that each party will have to contribute has not yet been determined.[19] In the late 1990s, however, then Prime Minister Hsiao Wan-chang proposed that the pension system should be implemented earlier, i.e. by July 1999, but fiscal restraints and the September 1999 earthquake delayed the implementation of the national pension system at least for a couple of years.[20]

The Development of Government Expenditures

The author of this book intently focused on a qualitative assessment of welfare state development in Taiwan first, and only now goes on to the discuss the expenditure statistics which, when studied alone, may give only limited knowledge on the changes in the course of welfare state development and, especially, the reasons behind them. The last two decades of Taiwanese welfare state development have witnessed a rather steady extension of government expenditures in the field of social welfare until 1994. After the introduction of the national health insurance in 1995, the cost for governmental social welfare increased a great deal, and so did the cost for retirement benefits for government employees. The expenditures for education, science and cultural affairs ranged between 17 and 20 percent of overall governmental expenditures. Though, total government expenditure between 1981 and 1999 increased by 491 percent, social welfare expenditures only grew by 355 percent. Interestingly, social welfare expenditures in 1999 surpassed that of economic affairs for the first time, marking the new importance of social policy in Taiwan politics. The expenditures for military and international affairs went down 10 percentage points, which is equal to the growth in social welfare expenditures (see Table 30).

When looking at the distribution of welfare expenditures on central government level, we notice again the jump in the cost for social insurance from the year 1994 to 1995; expenditures rose by 45.5 percent and reached 49.2 percentage points of all social welfare expenditures of the central government. From 1995 to 1999, the expenditures of social welfare services ranged between 36 and 41.8 percent. What is remarkable is the hefty increase in the spending for social relief, which surged by 337 percent from 1994 to 1999. Since health care expenditures became a the task of the National Health Insurance, health care expenditures other than for the NHI diminished and counted merely for 3.2 percent of total social welfare expenditures of the central government. Welfare state expenditure in the field of employment and vocational training continued to play a rather insignificant role in the Taiwanese welfare state system (see Table 31).

Taking the development of social welfare expenditures at different government levels, we see that there had been no radical changes, but a general trend is clear, i.e. a decrease in the financial responsibilities of the central government in comparison to county/city governments, as well as townships and villages. The total expenditure of all government levels for social welfare grew 27.29 percent in between 1995 and 1997, but then it decreased by 4.62 percent in the next two years, reaching 514.88 billion TWD in 1999.

Table 30: Net Government Expenditure, in billion TWD, percent (1981-1999)

Year	Total in bill. TWD	General Govern-mental Expendi-ture in %	Military and Inter-national Affairs in %	Eco-nomic Aff. in %	Social Wel-fare in %	Retire-ment Benefits for Gov't Employ-ees in %	Educa-tion, Science, Cultural Affairs in %	Commu-nity Dev't, Environ-mental Protection in %	Interest Pay-ments for Debts in %
1981	43.3	9.8	24.2	33.5	3.8	5.9	17.4	2.1	2.1
1986	63.2	11.1	24.2	24.4	6.4	6.8	20.4	2.5	3.4
1992	169.6	11.7	14.1	27.3	8.0	5.6	19.1	3.7	9.9
1993	185.9	11.2	13.6	29.4	7.8	5.5	18.9	3.9	9.0
1994	191.3	11.3	16.8	24.5	8.3	5.8	20.0	4.3	8.5
1995	207.4	10.7	13.0	21.1	11.2	5.7	17.2	3.1	17.3
1996	200.5	12.2	14.2	16.4	14.5	6.8	18.7	3.4	13.4
1997	206.6	11.8	14.1	14.3	14.3	8.7	18.2	3.3	14.7
1998	220.4	11.7	14.2	15.2	12.8	8.5	18.7	3.4	14.9
1999	212.7	12.9	12.5	13.3	13.5	9.2	20.1	3.2	13.7

Source: Hsiao-hung Nancy Chen (2000), 'Searching for Social Insurance Model(s): Taiwan's National Pension System in the Making', p. 9.

Table 31: Central Government's Social Welfare Expenditure's Structure (1994-1998)

Year	Growth rate in %	Total Expendi-ture in bill. TWD	Social Insurance in %	Welfare Services in %	Social Relief in %	Health Care in %	Employ-ment in %
1994	-	91.04	33.8	49.1	3.7	10.9	2.5
1995	47.7	134.46	49.2	36.0	7.1	6.2	1.5
1996	6.9	143.73	43.1	38.1	12.1	4.5	2.2
1997	4.4	150.02	41.7	41.8	10.4	3.7	2.4
1998	5.1	157.70	45.0	38.2	12.5	3.2	1.1

Source: Hsiao-hung Nancy Chen (2000), 'Searching for Social Insurance Model(s): Taiwan's National Pension System in the Making', p. 10.

The relative expenditures of central government and provincial government authorities in the area of social welfare fell by 3 percentage points each; that of Taipei city government grew by 2 percentage points, and that of

Kaohsiung and other county/city governments increased by 1 percentage point. Village and townships, most surprisingly, are experiencing a sizeable extension in their financial obligations in providing social welfare to its citizens, reaching 10.8 percent of total expenditures in the year 1998 (see Table 32).

Table 32: The Share of Social Welfare Expenditure at Different Government Levels (1995-1999)

Year	Total Exp-pendi-. ture in billion TWD	Central Govern -ment in %	Provin-cial Govern -ment in %	Taipei Muni-cipal Gov't in %	Kao-hsiung Muni-cipal Gov't in %	County Govern -ment in %	Village, Town-ship Gov't in %
1995	424.09	60.2	12.8	6.6	3.1	11.4	6.0
1996	496.73	54.8	18.1	8.2	3.1	9.9	5.9
1997	539.83	56.5	16.7	7.0	3.3	10.7	5.9
1998	543.73	56.5	14.4	8.3	3.6	10.8	10.8
1999	514.88	57.3	9.9	8.6	4.0	12.4	7.9

Source: Hsiao-hung Nancy Chen (2000), 'Searching for Social Insurance Model(s): Taiwan's National Pension System in the Making', p. 10.

In spite of all the recent changes after the introduction of democracy, the Taiwanese welfare state system caters, to an overwhelming extent, to privileged groups of society who had been selected by the Kuomintang government a long time ago (to secure its authoritarian and, later on, democratic rule). Traditionally, military servicemen and civil servants constituted the core of the Kuomintang's attention in social policy making; most resources were directed to this clientele. Teachers became another advantaged group in the 1980s due to their powerful status in society, i.e. potentially being able to either promote directly or indirectly public discontent, as well as – which was of interest to the KMT – to promote government propaganda.

The last, and by far largest, societal group that become beneficiaries of new KMT social policies were farmers and fishermen (see Table 33), due to their vast numbers and traditional conservative political orientations, this societal group was the one most suitable for electoral bribery by means of new, distributive social policies. The farmers' health insurance and the old farmers' allowance aimed at securing conservative votes for the KMT in upcoming national and local elections in the late 1980s and thereafter. Laborers were suppressed for a long time by the capitalist-thinking KMT; they formed key supporters for left wing parties, such as the Workers Party and the Labor Party. The labor faction of the DPP drew a great deal of supporters from the working population, especially since it strongly supported the formation of independent labor unions (others were firmly controlled and led by KMT officials). Before the year 1995, it were soldiers who benefited most from social welfare benefits, thereafter farmers (cf Yang, 1992: 102; and J.W. Xu, 1993: 47).

Bearing in mind the new importance of the masses for electoral victories in democratic elections, it is clear why the KMT had chosen farmers and fishermen in the mid-1990s to be the number one target in social policy making, giving them 13.27 times more social welfare benefits per capita than what was given to laborers (i.e. in 1995).

Table 33: The Distribution of Financial Resources of the Central Government's Budget for Benefits Received by Different Groups of Recipients in 1995

	Welfare Budget of Central Government, in TWD	Welfare Budget of Central Government, in %	Persons in Overall Population	Persons in Overall Population in %
Farmers and Fishermen	37,877,626	36.7	4,323,397	17.6
Military Servants	30,384,367	29.5	597,157	2.4
Civil Servants and Teachers	14,267,017	13.8	1,072,119	4.3
Elderly People	6,187,131	6.0	1,420,000	5.8
Laborers	5,744,787	5.6	8,703,000	35.5
Handicapped	3,958,451	3.8	241,144	1.0
Low-Income Earners	2,111,500	2.1	117,224	0.5
Children and the Youth	1,457,115	1.4	6,640,000	27.1
Women	155,318	0.1	1,420,000	5.8
Total	103,143,132	100	24,534,041	100

Source: Legislative Yuan (1997), 'Handicapped Benefits', p. 328.

Farmers and fishermen counted for 4.3 million people and 17.6 percent of all social expenditures of the central government were used for this group.

Military servants benefited most, counting only 2.4 percent of the population, they managed to extract most of welfare benefits from the central government's welfare budget, i.e. per capita, adding up to 29.5 percent of the social welfare budget. Civil servants and teachers also fared well; they secured 13.8 percent of welfare benefits, i.e. more than three times the share of population they represent.

The societal groups who had been notoriously neglected were women, children, the youth, as well as laborers. Low income-earners and the handicapped on the other hand only received an average proportion of the welfare pie, in proportional terms (cf Table 33).

Overall Changes in Taiwanese Social Policy

Social policy in the first three decades of postwar Taiwan was characterized by limited engagement of the then ruling Kuomintang in the domain of social welfare; most social policies aimed at the regulation and not the provision of social welfare. The comprehensive labor insurance system is the main piece of social legislation passed in this period, installing a labor insurance along the one the Communist Party of China has already implemented two years earlier in Manchuria, in the year 1948 (cf Aspalter, 2001a).

The Kuomintang never really had the implementation of a wide-ranging social insurance system in mind, the war with the Japanese and then with the Communists provided a good excuse for not setting up a social insurance system or any other vital social policies that were supported by the social thought of Dr. Sun Yat-sen, the founder of the Republic of China and the designer of its constitution. Why is there no valid excuse? Simply because the Communists implemented a labor insurance system during the heydays of the Civil War, even at a time they only controlled a part of China only, i.e. Northeastern China. Neither in the year 1911 and during the first years of the new republic – which experienced, indeed, difficult times in getting hold of all parts of the country – nor in the years of erecting the first powerful government following 1925, the Kuomintang showed serious attempts of constructing a welfare system in Mainland China. In 1928, the Kuomintang pronounced for the first time its intention to formulate a labor insurance law, but only six years later the Department of Industry of the Kuomintang government produced a draft version of the law. Again three years later in 1937, it declared the labor insurance law as one of its tasks for implementation (Chow and Xu, 2001: 131-2).

In 1950, then on Taiwan, the Kuomintang had to learn from its defeat on the mainland, and started to realize within the shortest possible time a labor insurance scheme, and a comprehensive land reform; all of which was paralleled by earlier efforts of the Communist Party in Mainland China. The reasons for the sudden change in KMT policymaking are, thus, more political and economical. Important Taiwanese scholars (e.g. Chan and Ying, 2001) tend to underestimate or neglect the factor of social policies of the People's Republic of China. Neither economic considerations – i.e. increasing the national saving rates (so that the government can borrow cheap money for investment in infrastructure or for financing its war/defense efforts) – nor increasing welfare needs due to the process of industrialization provided the reason for the sudden implementation of major social and societal policies of the KMT in the early 1950s.

From the 1950s to the 1970s, the KMT successfully limited the scope and the size of governmental social policies. It pursued social policies that reflected its situation of being in a quasi state of war with Mainland China. For the KMT the Civil War was lost for the moment, but in historical terms the ideological, economic and military battle for a possible (but very unlikely and, thus, theoretic) re-conquest of the mainland continued. Only in the 1990s with the change of politics of Lee Teng-hui, the KMT gave up its unrealistic dream of coming back to the mainland, as a ruling party.

The only booming sector in state welfare policies during the first three decades after the Civil War was social insurance for state employees, i.e. military and civil servants. The government set up the Government Employee Insurance and the Retired Government Employee Insurance in 1958 and 1965 respectively. In the early 1970s, the Kuomintang, in addition, was shaken by developments of the international political arena; especially the expulsion from the United Nations of which the Republic of China was a founding member; the massive withdrawal of diplomatic recognition of the ROC by Western countries; and, on top of that, the switching of diplomatic relations from Taipei to Beijing by the United States of America. Social policies of the 1970s reflect these changes a great deal. The Servicemen Insurance Provisions of 1970 preceded these political events, but social welfare benefits for military servicemen had been extended mainly after 1972. New retirement benefits and insurance, new housing programs and health care benefits, and new benefits in the field of family income maintenance for military servicemen had been introduced in the subsequent years (see Table 34).

In the 1980s, the pressure for introducing new governmental social policies augmented and changed from being externally caused by international factors to being internally caused by social discontent geared by Taiwan's growing opposition movement. While continuing to extend the coverage of labor insurance, which did not present a burden for the national budget – but rather had positive effects for the economy and the government – since it is a contributory insurance scheme, the government extended state welfare arrangements to new privileged groups, these were: employees of private schools (the Insurance Provisions for Teachers and Employees of Private Schools in 1980); retired government employees (Health Insurance for Retired Government Employees in 1985); family members of active and retired government employees (two health insurance schemes, in 1982 and 1985); and family members of active and retired employees of private schools (two health insurance schemes, in 1985 and 1989).

Table 34: The Change of the Content of Social Policies in Taiwan

Prior to 1972	1972-1976	1977-1988	1989-1994	1995 to present
1. Education 2. Civil Servants' Retirement Benefits and Insurance 3. Social Relief 4. Health 5. Employ-ment 6. Housing	1. Education 2. Civil Servants, Military Servicemen Retirement Benefits & Insurance 3. Veterans' Settlement and Health Care 4. Military Servicemen Family Income Maintenance 5. Social Relief 6. Health 7. Employ-ment 8. Housing	1. Education 2. Retirement Benefits and Insurance, especially for employees of state institutions and private schools 3. Social Relief 4. Health 5. Employ-ment 6. Housing	1. Education 2. Welfare Services 3. Social Insurance (including retirement benefits) 4. Health Care 5. Social Relief 6. Employ-ment 7. Public Housing & Community Development 8. Environ-mental Protection	1. Social Insurance (including pension, health and unemploy-ment insurance) 2. Education 3. Welfare Services 4. Social Relief 5. Health Care 6. Employment 7. Community Development 8. Environ-mental Protection

Sources: based on Hsiao-hung Nancy Chen (2000), 'Searching for Social Insurance Model(s): Taiwan's National Pension System in the Making', pp. 2, 9, 10; Bai Hsiu-hsiung (1980), 'Rui Dian Mei Guo Ji Wo Guo She Hui Fu Li Bi Jiao Yan Jiou', pp. 412-28; and Council for Economic Planning and Development (1996), 'She Hui Fu Li Zhi Zhu Dui Cong Ti Jing Ji Fa Zhan Zhi Ying Xiang', p. 21.

The introduction of the farmers' health insurance in 1989, after having run pilot programs for four years, marked the beginning of a new era in Taiwanese welfare state politics in which social policy was the outcome of the new party system and democratic elections. In the same year, the government created a health insurance scheme for local representatives, heads of villages, districts, and all levels of the provincial government, as well as that of the self-governing cities, Taipei and Kaohsiung. The motivation behind the implementation of these first two major social insurance schemes is an obvious one: the KMT wanted and needed to win elections. It was highly concerned about the early massive successes of the newly formed Democratic Progressive Party in the first democratic elections of postwar Taiwan. In 1991, the KMT, for the first time set up a special social insurance scheme for needy groups, that is the Health Insurance for the Disabled and Handicapped. In addition, the government started to emphasize welfare services, since competitive providers of social services emerged, i.e. non-governmental welfare organizations that were highly organized and important grass-root organizations affiliated with, or closely tied via personal ties to the Democratic Progressive Party.

In the 1990s, the importance of community development, as well as new issues such as unemployment and environmental protection, became pivotal concerns of policymakers (Table 34). With the implementation of the National Health Insurance in 1995 and the Unemployment Benefit scheme of the Labor Insurance, Taiwanese social policy entered a new era of extended welfare policies based on large-scale, contributory insurance schemes. Only pension benefits are offered by the Labor Insurance scheme. The implementation of the National Pension Insurance had been postponed due to fiscal constraints. But on local level, the DPP implemented new non-contributory, universal old-age allowance schemes (i.e. universal pensions). The Taiwanese welfare state system has been transformed from a residual, rudimentary to a substantially extended residual welfare state. With every year Taiwan approaches the size and the extent of Western welfare state systems. The rapid extension of Taiwanese welfare state system is far from being completed and can be expected to continue in the years and decades to come.

5 The Impact of the 1997 Elections on Social Policy

DPP Wins more Votes than KMT for the First Time in an Island-wide Election:[21] Results and their Implications

The elections for city mayors and county commissioners on November 29, 1997 were not simply regional elections. They can be seen as a sample of what lies ahead in the upcoming general elections in 1998. President Lee Teng-hui said that these elections represented a battle for local control that 'could affect our party's overall power base'.[22] His prediction came true. The KMT lost in all important counties and cities, and the DPP, won a landslide victory.

The DPP won in twelve out of the 23 counties in which elections were held. The twelve counties and cities won by the DPP constitute 71.53 percent of the population of Taiwan (including its small outer islands, i.e., Penghu, Kinmen and Lienchiang counties).[23] Thus, elected DPP members represented 15.5 million out of 21 and a half million Taiwanese. The KMT won only in eight counties and lost in all five participating cities. The eight counties in which the Kuomintang retained power largely make up the least-populated rural provinces of Taiwan, such as Taitung, Hualien, Yunlin, or represent small outer islands. The population in the eight counties won by the Kuomintang adds up, all together, to only 2.3 million voters. Taipei county, the largest county (won by DPP) alone has 2.24 million voters. The counties and cities in which DPP candidates were elected in 1997 comprised 8.6 million voters.[24]

This island-wide victory for the DPP in that year marks a new era in Taiwan politics. Since the majority of votes were polled by the DPP in 1997 – i.e., 43.5 percent compared to 42.1 percent[25] for the KMT – the victory also in parliamentary election was not a long time in coming; in fact, the 2001 parliamentary election, indeed, brought a changeover of power, after 51 years of KMT rule in Taiwan.

However, what most observers have not noticed is that the KMT lost its majority in the Lower House of parliament (the Legislative Yuan) quite some time ago.[26] This happened after Hsiao Wan-chang had to give back his seat after becoming Prime Minister in the last cabinet led by the KMT. In addition, legislator Lin Chih-chia was then expelled from the party for running against the party's nominee in the Taipei county commissioner elections on November 29, leaving the KMT with only 80 of 162 seats in 1997.[27] Lin Chih-chia resigned as a member of parliament in order to show his 'do or die' commitment to winning the position of county chief.[28] After the November 29 by-elections in Chiayi city for the empty seat of Hsiao Wan-chang, the DPP candidate, Trong Chai, took the seat from the KMT. Thus, the KMT could not hope to retain a majority (82 seats).

In view of the 1997 election results that were highly in favor of the DPP, the future of the KMT seemed to be rather gloomy. The KMT now had to fight against – what seemed impossible before the 1997 elections – that is, the risk of becoming an opposition party. The twelve elected DPP county commissioners and city mayors could consolidate the support of their party. Once they manage to govern their counties and cities to the voters' satisfaction, their chances of being re-elected are high. In the 1997 elections, seven out of eight ruling county commissioners who sought re-election were successful (four from the KMT and three from the DPP). Only the KMT commissioner in Miaoli county lost. He had been too sure of winning the election and had failed to promote his election campaign sufficiently.[29] Considering the advantage now held by DPP members, it was extremely difficult for the KMT to win back seats lost to the DPP (six) and to independent candidates (two). In 2001, the KMT only could win back one seat, however, the DDP lost three.[30]

The Issue of Old-age Allowances

Old-age allowances were the overriding issue in the campaign for county and city mayor elections on November 29, in 1997. The topic had first been promoted by the DPP in the county and city mayor elections four years previously. Nevertheless, the DPP had not intended to focus on old-age benefits again as it had no wish to draw attention to its own failure to provide such allowances (i.e., TWD 5,000[31] per month per person over 65 years[32] of age).[33] However, Hsieh Shen-shan backed by Lee Teng-hui forced the issue by launching a new old-age allowance campaign for the KMT in Taipei. Lee said that if the KMT candidate for Taipei county (Hsieh Shen-shan) were elected county commissioner, every person over 65 would receive 5,000 TWD dollars a month – all year round. DPP's former Taipei county commissioner, You Ching, had also made a similar promise in 1993, but in the event could only provide stipends for four months owing to a lack of funds.

The DPP's old-age allowance proposal four years previously had been heavily reliant on the unlikely – and unexpected – support of the central and provincial governments. Indeed, financial support was refused by these government authorities. In all counties and cities won by the DPP – and Chiayi city which an independent candidate won – old-age allowances were introduced. However, in most cases these payments had to be stopped after four months. The official reason for the termination of old-age allowance payments was that the central and provincial governments were each supposed to contribute one-third of the funds. This money was not forthcoming which left the DPP with only enough resources for four months.[34] Richer cities and counties can rely on higher revenues from local business and land taxes.[35]

Only in wealthy Hsinchu county did old-age allowances continue throughout the year. In Taipei city, also wealthy, the old-age benefit payments lasted seven months before the city council discontinued them due to 'financial constraints'.[36] The DPP's attitude towards old-age allowances was that when money was readily available they would be paid out. When funds were scarce then it was not priority issue (tax increases are taboo in general).

The DPP's commitment to social welfare was attacked by the President in the Taipei county election campaign. On the subject Lee Teng-hui said '... some people just go half-way, three or four months, and then say there's no money. That's all a lie. They dare to say this even though the money is there. It's impossible for them to handle things with compassion and care.'[37] With Lee Teng-hui's support of Hsieh Shen-shan's old-age allowance proposal, the issue of granting allowances to the elderly became prominent in the November 29 elections throughout Taiwan, and even forced the DPP to return, in response, to this topic.

National Approach to Old-age Allowances

In early November, the DPP proposed a stipend bill for the elderly in the Lower House of parliament (The Legislative Yuan).[38] This proposal would have speeded up the introduction of a nation-wide stipend system. The DPP pushed the stipend bill directly into the second-reading review process. However, it was rejected by 46 to 73 votes. The KMT and the New Party opposed the proposal because they feared that a DPP success so close to polling day might favor them on county level. The KMT also opposed the DPP's bill because it insisted on upholding its policy that old-age allowances should remain a local issue.

The New Party did not back the national old-age allowance bill as it was considered to be too hurried. The New Party's caucas chief, Chou Yang-shan, defended his party's opposition to the bill saying his party wanted to plan the welfare program in detail before implementing it. The KMT intended to present its own proposal for locally administered senior citizens' stipends after the November 29 elections (thus KMT lawmaker Yao Ying-chi). Chen Ding-nan, the DPP caucas chief, said that by introducing the bill the DPP was trying to respond to President Lee's and Hsieh Shen-shan's promotion of old-age allowances in Taipei county. The Provincial Governor James Soong regarded the stipend program as 'unfeasible' due to the nation's financial condition.[39] Moreover, James Soong told the Taiwan Provincial Assembly that he could not be convinced of the need to give the stipend to some of the richest senior citizens in Taiwan.[40]

Essentially, both the KMT and DPP are trying to implement a national solution to the problem of benefits to the elderly. Although none of the three major parties rejects social welfare for the elderly, there are some major differences between party proposals. In the KMT white paper on old-age allowances in 1997 a new general principle was put forward stating that all people over 70 years should receive 3,000 TWD dollars every month. Moreover, the elderly in middle and low-income families and the elderly disabled or sick are eligible for extra allowances. The KMT's opinion regarding old-age benefits was that counties with better financial capabilities could provide more benefits than other counties.[41] The old-age allowance system should be able to bridge the gap between current social needs and social welfare for the elderly before the introduction of the national pension system.

The DPP wanted to establish the old-age allowance system, contrary to the KMT, on the national level. Furthermore, the DPP proposed that the system of old-age allowances should be flexible depending on the financial resources that are available at the time, i.e., a quasi stop-and-go formula. The New Party proposed a different solution, offering to support three-generation households rather than pay old-age allowances to the elderly. This new 'lao qin lu tie' policy proposed to subsidize three-generation households under the precondition that all three generations live together. These families should receive TWD 20,000 annually. The Taiwan Independence Party supported the DPP proposal that old-age allowances should be consistent throughout Taiwan.[42]

Chan Hou-sheng (KMT) was one of the first to address the problem of raising funds to support the old-age allowance schemes promised during the election campaign. According to Chan Hou-sheng, the introduction of comprehensive allowance schemes would have two major results. First, other social services have to be cut, and second, taxes have to be increased. Otherwise, it is 'almost impossible' to sustain both these programs and honor election promises.[43]

County Level Proposals for Old-age Allowances

The people of other counties felt that the KMT regarded them as inferior to privileged Taipei county citizens. Lee Teng-hui's proposal triggered a chain reaction in local politics. Other KMT candidates were forced by their voters either to propose similar plans (in Miaoli) or to advocate a nation-wide old-age allowance system (in Changhua).[44] In Ilan county where old-age allowances were previously only paid out for four months, the KMT candidate, Liao Feng-teh, promised that he would pay out a minimum of TWD 3,000 per month to the elderly.[45] The KMT candidate for Taichung city promised to give every citizen over 65 years of age TWD 5,000 per month if he were elected and if Taipei county went ahead with its old-age allowance scheme. He did not want Taichung residents to feel they were 'second-class citizens' by comparison.[46]

Kaohsiung mayor Wu Den-yih challenged the attitude of President Lee when he questioned the use of the old-age allowance program as a major campaign issue. In the 1994 Kaoshiung mayoral campaign, his opponent from the DPP had promised a monthly TWD 5,000 stipend for the elderly citizens. Wu Den-yih said that despite the fact that he had not made any old-age allowance promise that year, he had still been elected. Wu noted, 'I decided not to touch the (stipend) issue. But the Kaoshiung residents loved me and I got elected.'

In response, President Lee said, 'Of course you're lucky. You got elected. But this year's situation is different.'[47] Lee, furthermore, stated that Wu Den-yih stood little chance of re-election in the 1998 Kaoshiung mayoral election.[48] Wu then said that he would agree to the stipend program if there was sound financial planning and if it covered the whole of Taiwan rather than single county and city magistrates.[49] A survey for the KMT reported that a large proportion of the electorate (approximately 30 to 40 percent) was influenced by the issue of old-age allowances. In order to win the support of the entire electorate, i.e. all social welfare interest groups, such as women and youth, other issues needed to be focused on as well.[50]

Sissy Chen, the then spokeswoman of the DPP, considered old-age allowances to be highly influential in Hsinchu city and county, Nantou county, Yunlin county, Chiayi county and Pingtung county.[51] In Hsinchu, the elderly have already received old-age allowances, without interruption, for the last four years. Therefore, maintaining old-age allowances had become a necessity in order to win the county commissioner and city mayor elections. Both the KMT and the DPP constantly accused one another of being half-hearted in matters concerning social welfare for the elderly. Chen Hong-jih, the KMT party whip, said that the DPP had not successfully implemented the old-age allowance system since the last elections for city mayors and county magistrates, in 1993 and 1994 respectively.

In the wake of the November 1997 election campaign – pressured by President Lee's support of Hsieh Shen-shan's proposal for old-age allowances in Taipei county – the DPP promoted the issue once more in order to remain competitive, which indeed proved vital for its victory. Chen Hong-jih criticized the DPP for being too hasty. The DPP countered that the KMT had proved that it was not credible because it had opposed the two senior citizens' stipend bills raised by the DPP in parliament while claiming to support the elderly.[52]

Representatives from all major political camps continued to accuse one another of engaging in some kind of vote-buying by discussing old-age allowance proposals. Lin Chih-chia (ex-KMT legislator and independent candidate in Taipei county) characterized Lee Teng-hui's announcement as 'not extremely responsible, a somewhat underhanded way of vote-buying'. Only days earlier, Tsai Pi-huang, the KMT spokesman, had made similar accusations against the DPP. In addition, the United Evening News cited an official party magazine of the KMT thus: 'The pension policy promoted by the DPP in this county's elections is clearly a trick to get votes, it is the greatest lie and biggest ruse of this century, this is a policy to buy votes, the KMT would never do anything like this.'[53]

The Importance of Old-age Allowances for the November 29 Elections

Candidates from all political camps, either party affiliated or running as independents, put forward the issue of social welfare. Owing to Lee Teng-hui's commitment in the elections, old-age allowances became the overriding issue for most. The majority of the 80 candidates in the county commissioner and city mayor elections, i.e. 42 candidates (52.5 percent), promoted the topic of social welfare intensively and among them 32 candidates offered a variety of old-age allowance proposals to the electorate. Old-age allowances paid out at special Chinese festivals were offered by three candidates, two of whom were subsequently elected. Other kinds of old-age allowances to be paid out monthly were put forward by 29 candidates.

Ten other candidates promised other social welfare programs, e.g. some kind of education allowance for schoolchildren, birth allowances, etc. According to the public circular, the 'gong bao',[54] the welfare policies of 20 other candidates were rather limited and vague. The election manifestos contained statements such as 'taking care of the elderly' or 'promoting social welfare'. The remaining 18 candidates promoted major topics other than social welfare (Table 35).

Table 35: Social Welfare Policies of all Candidates in the November 29 Elections

Category	Social policy	No.
Old-age allowance at festivals	a main topic	3
Monthly old-age allowance	a main topic	29
Other social policies only	a main topic	10
Vague commitment	a small topic	20
No major social policies	a minor topic	18
Total		80

Since there were 80 candidates in 23 constituencies, the chances of becoming elected were on average slightly better than one to four. The chances of election victory through the heavy promotion of the social welfare issue were one to three, as 14 out of 42 candidates who supported social policies were elected. More than half of the elected candidates had a strong social policy interest (i.e., 14 out of 23). Seven others also supported social welfare, but it was not their main focus (Table 36).

Table 36: Elected Candidates and their Social Welfare Policy

Candidates	Social welfare is main topic	Social welfare is a small topic[55]	Social welfare is a minor topic[56]
Elected	14	7	2
Newly elected	10	4	1
Re-elected	4	3	1
Not re-elected		1	

Only two successful candidates did not emphasize social policies in the hot phase of the election campaign: Annette Lu (DPP) in Taoyuan county focused on the issue of environmental protection and the garbage problem. Liao Yung-lai (DPP) in Taichung county emphasized infrastructural development and the anti-Bayer campaign.[57] Both DPP politicians are pro-welfare, but in that election campaign they concentrated on other more controversial issues in these elections.

Table 37: The History of Old-age Allowances in the Last Election Period[58]

Party	Constituency	Original proposal	Factual payments, 1993 to 1997	Situation in 1997
DPP	Ilan county	NT 5,000	NT 3,000; each year 4 months	continued
DPP	Taipei county	NT 5,000	each year 4 months	continued
DPP	Taoyuan county	NT 2,000	at three festivals per year	continued
DPP	Hsinchu county	NT 5,000	each month	continued
DPP	Tainan county	NT 5,000 & NT 2,500	4 months 1995: TWD 3,000 & TWD 1,000 1996: every New Year TWD 2,000 & subsidy to health insurance premium monthly TWD 233	every New Year TWD 2,000 & health insurance premium subsidy TWD 233 per month
DPP	Kaoshiung county	NT 5,000	4 months then stopped	stopped
DPP	Penghu county	NT 5,000	each month TWD 3,000	continued
Indep.	Chiayi city	NT 5,000	4 months then stopped	stopped
DPP	Tainan city	NT 1,000	each month 1996: only 9 months TWD 2,000 1997: 6 months TWD 500 then stopped	stopped
DPP	Taipei city	NT 5,000	7 months then stopped	stopped

If a candidate already held the position of county commissioner or city mayor, this had a significant influence on the outcome of these elections. Being the chief of the county or city government was a real advantage for being re-elected, as mentioned earlier.

Only one candidate (KMT) in Miaoli county was not re-elected as he had taken his victory for granted and had not therefore participated actively enough in the election campaign.[59] The other eight candidates who were standing for election a second time were re-elected.

The majority of the elected candidates who concentrated on social policies was newly elected (i.e., 10 out of 14) and therefore could not rely on the advantage of previous candidacy. The eight candidates who were re-elected (five KMT and three DPP) showed no significant bias towards social policy. Only two of them promoted old-age allowances, two promoted other social policies, three made weaker commitments to social welfare and one did not emphasize social welfare at all. Only the number of candidates who made strong commitments to social policy fell behind the overall average.

The experience of broken election promises in the previous four years (cf Table 37) had changed the view of many voters and candidates. Nonetheless, Yu Cheng-hsien (DPP candidate from Kaoshiung county) and Chen Tang-shan (DPP candidate from Tainan county) were re-elected in these November 29 elections, as was Annette Lu (DPP candidate from Taoyuan county).

The electorate did not forget the campaign promises, especially in Kaoshiung county where they remained largely unfulfilled.[60] Chen Tang-shan honored his promise longer than did Yu Cheng-hsien. After one or two changes to benefits, the people in Tainan county still received TWD 2,000 once a year at the New Year Festival and TWD 233 for the monthly national health insurance contribution. Annette Lu, on the contrary, had not promised more than she could give to the people of Taoyuan county. Her overwhelming election result (56.2 percent) confirmed the voters' approval. On the contrary, new candidates in Tainan city, Chiayi city, Penghu county and Kaoshiung county had to bear the brunt of broken election promises of the year 1993.

The new candidates running for election in the first three counties had better chances of reaching the electorate. Failure by DPP candidates and the independent candidate to honor the promises made in the earlier election certainly influenced the elections. It is because of these broken election promises that the DPP did not originally want to promote the issue of old-age allowances a second time. On county and city level, it is clear that many different factors contributed to the success of certain candidates or parties (cf Table 38).

Table 38: Losses and Gains in the November 29 Elections Compared to 1993[61]

	KMT 1993	KMT 1997	Win/ Loss	DPP 1993	DPP 1997	Win/ Loss	Others 1993	Others 1997	Win/ Loss
Taipei county	**35.97**	**38.67**	**2.7**	**46.38**	**40.67**	-5.71	17.65	20.66	3.01
Taoyuan county[62]	39.32	42.96	3.64	**36.27**	**56.2**	**19.93**	24.41	0.84	-23.57
Pingtung county	50.93	41.45	-9.48	**48.16**	**55.42**	**7.26**	0.91	3.13	2.22
Kaoshiung county	47.11	44.69	-2.42	**51.31**	**51.74**	**0.43**	1.58	3.57	1.99
Taichung city	**58.13**	**41.28**	**-16.85**	**41.87**	**49.57**	**7.7**	0	9.15	9.15
Changhua county	52.81	49.56	-3.25	**40.84**	**48.66**	**7.82**	6.35	1.78	-4.57
Tainan county	42.85	34.27	-8.58	**53.99**	**65.73**	**11.74**	3.16	0	-3.16
Miaoli county	33.58	35.37	1.79	25.4	4.17	-21.23	41.02	**60.46**	19.44
Chiayi city	43.22	42.52	-0.7	0	5.45	5.45	56.78	**52.03**	-4.75
Keelung city	**54.66**	**37.97**	**-16.69**	45.34	42.75	-2.59	0	**19.28**	19.28
Ilan county	40.41	46.17	5.76	**57.49**	**53.83**	**-3.66**	2.1	0	-2.1
Hsinchu county	43.25	32.89	-10.36	50.04	36.12	-13.92	6.71	**30.99**	24.28
Hsinchu city	55.13	42.79	-12.34	**26.88**	**56.11**	**29.23**	17.99	1.1	-16.89
Nantou county	49.54	30.11	-19.43	21.48	30.8	9.32	28.98	**39.09**	10.11
Hualien county	60.31	56.76	-3.55	**30.68**	**43.24**	**12.56**	9.01	0	-9.01
Taichung county[63]	**58.89**	**53.59**	-5.3	41.11	**37.6**	-3.51	0	8.81	8.81
Yunlin county	53.12	34.93	-18.19	46.88	29.11	-17.77	0	**35.96**	35.96
Tainan city[64]	46.13	38.78	-7.35	**30.28**	**35.75**	**5.47**	23.59	25.47	1.88
Chiayi county	66.4	53.26	-13.14	**33.19**	**46.74**	**13.55**	0.41	0	-0.41
Taitung county	68.57	47.64	-20.93	0	5.73	5.73	31.43	**46.63**	15.2
Penghu county	**42.44**	**57.53**	**15.08**	57.56	42.48	-15.08	0	0	0
Kinmen county		**58.61**		0	0	0		**41.39**	
Lienchiang county		**61**		0	0	0		**39**	

In Taipei county President Lee Teng-hui supported the proposal to pay out old-age allowances for the entire year, not just for the few months during which it was actually paid out by the former DPP county government.

Though in the lead at the start of the campaign, Su Zhen-chang (DPP) lost more and more ground to his opponent from the KMT, Hsieh Shen-shan. Hsieh Shen-shan was at a disadvantage vis-a-vis Lin Chih-chia (former KMT) because, not having been nominated by the KMT, he was running as an independent candidate. Lin Chih-chia polled more than 154,000 votes in Taipei county, winning them not only in the camp of the New Party (which performed badly) but also taking away essential votes from Hsieh Shen-shan.

In the two months before polling day, the electorate began to support Hsieh Shen-shan a great deal more. This is directly related to his proposal of paying allowances to the elderly because the KMT electorate in Taipei county is significantly older than that of the DPP. Soldiers and their wives who came to Taiwan in the late 1940s make up most of the older KMT electorate.

However, Hsieh Shen-shan lost the race on the eve of the election owing to Lu Shiu-yi. Originally, Lu should have run as the DPP candidate in Taipei county, but at the time of his nomination he was diagnosed with cancer. He had already shown significant signs of his illness when, on the evening before the election, he went down on his knees in front of an emotionally overwhelmed electorate exhorting them to vote for his friend Su Zhen-chang. Lu Shiu-yi was then legislator and an important member of the DPP.

The ubiquitous news reports showing Lu Shiu-yi on his knees with tears in his eyes asking his audience to support Su Zhen-chang were the decisive factor. A few days before the election, the public and leading DPP members started to believe in the victory of Hsieh Shen-shan who led most polls.[65] 'To me, the continuous reporting of Lu's action was the main reason I was unable to get more swing votes than Su,' said Hsieh Shen-shan.[66] The KMT lost in Panchiao, the major city in Taipei county, where the incident happened. Also in Sanchung, the second important city, which was visited by Lu Shiu-yi and Chen Shui-bian the same evening. The missing 28,142 votes for the KMT were mainly lost in Sanchung (28,024 votes less than DPP) and Panchiao (16,467 votes less)[67] because in these two cities the candidates had received equal support from among the voters just a few days before the election.[68]

It can be noted that Hsieh Shen-shan won a great deal of votes, even surpassing Su Zhen-chang in the days before the election, due to a campaign that heavily emphasized the issue of old-age allowance. In the case of Taipei county, it can be shown that the DPP won in the cities and towns with the lowest share of elderly over 65. The KMT, by contrast, won in those cities and towns with a significantly higher share of elderly in the population. In this case study the author took the 17 most populated districts (from a total of 25 districts) in Taipei county, each of which has more than 10,000 eligible voters. The proportion of people over 65 in the population in the table below suggests the relative importance of old-age allowances for the KMT electorate because the KMT-dominated districts have significantly more old people than those clearly dominated by the DPP.

Table 39: The Significant Relationship Between Age-Structure and Party Dominance in Taipei County[69]

City/town	Population over 65		Majority of votes	Vote index	Population	Population density
	in %	in words[70]		Su/Hsieh	in 1,000	persons/km^2
Panchiao city	5.1	low	DPP	1.56	530	22,884
Sanchung city	4.9	very low	DPP	1.20	380	23,295
Yunghe city	**7.7**	**very high**	KMT	**0.67**	233	40,793
Chunghe city	**6.4**	**normal**	**KMT**	**0.76**	386	19,179
Hsinchuang city	3.2	lowest	DPP	1.4	339	17,139
Hsintien city	**9.2**	**highest**	**KMT**	**0.65**	251	2,084
Tucheng city	4.0	very low	DPP	1.2	188	6,371
Shulin town	4.1	very low	DPP	1.41	135	4,085
Sanhsia town	7.9	very high	DPP	1.06	70	366
Tanshui town	**6.8**	**high**	**KMT**	**0.67**	97	1,376
Hsichun town	**6.5**	**normal**	**KMT**	**0.88**	119	1,670
Luchou town	3.9	lowest	DPP	1.62	139	18,658
Wugu town	5.5	low	DPP	1.24	57	1,635
Taishan town	4.3	very low	DPP	1.06	60	3,108
Linkou town	6.2	normal	DPP	1.19	41	761
Sanchih town	**10.1**	**highest**	**KMT**	**0.33**	19	291
Pali town	**6.7**	**high**	**KMT**	**0.87**	22	565

The influence of other candidates on the election results was also important. Liao Xue-guang was the former mayor of Hsichun[71] and is loved by the people of Hsichun. He had been sentenced to 18 years in prison because he had illegally attempted to introduce a new tax for mostly non-local companies, which profited from a major highway project in Hsichun town. But as he was elected MP (with most votes island-wide, about 90,000) he did not have to serve the sentence.[72] In short, he is a local hero in Hsichun, which explains his high share of votes in that town. Lin Chih-chia won over-proportionally in the towns of Wugu, Taishan and Linkou, hence preventing an overall KMT majority. Lin was a former KMT politician and therefore a second good choice for traditional KMT voters. The same is true of Liao Xue-guang who came from the DPP camp.

Figure 1: The Dependence of the KMT on the Elderly in Taipei County[73]

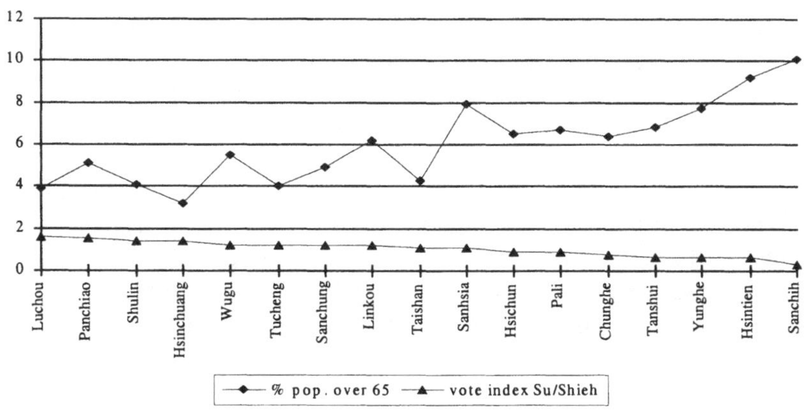

Bearing the influences of other candidates in mind, we can now look at the relationship between votes and the age structure in Taipei county districts. The following chart shows the 17 largest of the 25 districts. The DPP won the majority of votes in those districts with a significantly lower share of people over the age of 65. The KMT, on the contrary, won in those districts that have a higher proportion of elderly people in the population. This fact ultimately persuaded the KMT to promote social welfare for the elderly because the elderly constitute a large share of the party's specific electorate (see Table 39).

Lee Teng-hui was certainly an additional vote magnet for Hsieh, but so too was Chen Shui-bian for Su. The issue of old-age allowances was also subsequently put forward by Su Zhen-chang at Hsieh's proposal. It can be concluded that the KMT originally enjoyed popularity among the elderly (in Taipei county and probably also elsewhere) and/or the KMT won the support of the elderly owing to the election promises made by Hsieh and Lee (see Figure 1).

Nevertheless, the most important conclusion here is that the KMT was forced to promise more social welfare to their electorate due to intense party competition and the age structure of the KMT electorate. This can be clearly seen in Figure 1. In the districts in which Su Zhen-chang (DPP) won less votes than Hsieh Shen-shan (KMT) the share of the elderly over 65 is significantly higher than in those districts in which Su won more votes than Hsieh.

This has become especially clear in the case of social welfare for the elderly. The social policy of the KMT matched the demographic structure of its electorate in Taipei county. However, there is no doubt that the main reason for the promotion of old-age allowances by the KMT was the pressure to win the elections, a fact which is underlined by the timing of the launching of this program and by the comments of KMT politicians. For President Lee Teng-hui and Hsieh Shen-shan it was clear that they only had a chance of winning the election in Taipei county by promising to pay old-age benefits for an entire year.

The KMT had introduced the issue of old-age allowances in Taipei county because it has more financial resources and because it is the county with by far the largest population in Taiwan. In terms of voters, Taipei county was thus of crucial significance for the KMT in the November 29 elections. The overall importance of Taipei county is its size which is the main reason for the heavy promotion of social welfare for the elderly, not the proportion of elderly and/or the migration rate in Taipei county. In fact, the share of elderly over 65 in Taipei county was 5.88 percent in 1995, compared to 7.63 percent island-wide. Moreover, the migration rates among the primary metropolitan areas in Taiwan, i.e. Taipei, Kaoshiung, Taichung, Tainan and Taoyuan, resemble each other and do not provide a fundamental reason for discrimination between these areas in the question of social welfare for the elderly as well.[74]

In the case of Taoyuan county, it should be pointed out that Annette Lu promised TWD 2,000 old-age allowances three times a year and did not break this promise. She resolved the acute garbage problem to the satisfaction of the electorate during her short stint as Taoyuan county commissioner (since March 1997). Annette Lu has been, for a long time, a key player in Taiwan politics; she was imprisoned for six years because she gave a public speech during the Kaohsiung Incident in 1979. These are the main reasons for the Annette Lu's overwhelming absolute majority.

Another political rival in Taoyuan county, Hsu Yun-teh, founded the Social Reform Party on August 8 the same year. He proposed the highest old-age allowance, i.e., TWD 6,000 to 10,000 per month. Hsu Yun-teh saw his party not only as a party for the Hakka minority, but as a party for all small and weak groups with little political clout. The Social Reform Party aimed to decrease the gap between the rich and the poor and to promote overall social welfare.[75] Hsu promised support for children and the unemployed and poor. He noted that the Hakka minority was disproportionally affected by unemployment and poverty.[76] In Chungli, the second largest city in Taoyuan county, the Hakka minority constitutes the majority of the electorate. It was in Chungli and its southern and western neighboring districts that Hsu Yun-teh won significantly more votes (i.e., always more than one percent) than in the northern and eastern part of Taoyuan county. The overall result is 0.84 percent (5,619 votes), which may seem rather meager. Taking into account that the Social Reform Party was only founded little more than two and a half months before the election and that the other candidates, by contrast, spent hundreds of millions of TWD dollars on their election campaigns,[77] Hsu's debut performance was quite impressive.

In Kaoshiung county, Yu Cheng-hsien also managed to hold his absolute majority of votes, although he had been unable to honor his election promise of monthly old-age allowances. After paying out four months of allowances in 1994, he had had to discontinue the scheme owing to a lack of financial resources. Protests at the termination of the payments did not, however, mean the loss of Yu's absolute majority. Yu Cheng-hsien simply said: 'it is not possible' and that there were other ways of spreading wealth around; also that it would be a waste of resources as many of the elderly were wealthy and did not need old-age allowances. Yu's alternative approach envisaged insurance for children from birth until kindergarten entrance and compensation for hospitalization and death of a child up to the age of six. Furthermore, those men currently serving in the army were also covered by this kind of insurance.[78] Even though Yu Cheng-hsien had been unable to keep his old-age allowance promise, he had managed to implement important welfare policies and thus secure the votes of those concerned. Here lay the reason for the ongoing strong support of Yu that secured his second absolute majority in four years.

In Tainan county, Chen Tang-shan was confronted with the promises which he had made four years previously and which he had been unable to honor. The initial old-age allowance had been TWD 5,000 for normal elderly people and TWD 2,500 for soldiers, officials and teachers who already benefited disproportionally from existing welfare arrangements and insurance schemes. This level of old-age allowances, however, could only be maintained for four months. In the next year, 1995, benefits were reduced to TWD 3,000 for normal elderly and TWD 1,000 for soldiers, officials and teachers. The following year, only a New Year's old-age allowance of TWD 2,000 and a monthly subsidy of TWD 233 for contributions to the national health insurance remained from the once generous offer in 1993. Nonetheless, the people in Tainan county were obviously satisfied with Chen Tang-shan and gave him the highest support island-wide, i.e., 65.73 percent of votes. This was to a considerable extent a consequence of the welfare policies he had implemented and the people's confidence in Chen Tang-shan's future welfare measures.[79]

In Tainan city, the DPP candidate George Chang heavily played the card of social welfare as well. He promised to pay the health insurance premiums of children under three years and the elderly over 65. Moreover, he again promoted old-age allowances, i.e. monthly TWD 5,000 for those over 65 years of age between four to twelve months each year. In addition, George Chang promised an education allowance of TWD 3,000. Of the seven candidates for Tainan city (which is the highest number of candidates in these elections) only George Chang focused on the policy of granting old-age allowances. The two KMT candidates only made vague statements like 'taking care of the elderly'.

The fourth candidate with a chance of election victory, Hsu Tien-tsai (an independent candidate), was the only other proponent of social welfare policies. His plan was to pay the health insurance premiums of children under three and the elderly over 65.[80] George Chang also had a trump card in the person of Chen Shui-bian, who supported him strongly in his election campaign.[81] Chen, the current Taipei city mayor, is a hero in the eyes of most DPP voters. It is for these two major reasons that George Chang had victory on his side. In Tainan city, two candidates were nominated by the KMT. Some observers suggested that by adding both results the KMT would have won. However, this was only true in Taichung county, where there were also two KMT candidates. In Tainan city, there was an independent candidate, Hsu Tien-tsai, who was both a previous member of the DPP and a former classmate of Taipei city mayor Chen Shui-bian.[82] This made Hsu very popular with the DPP electorate and he took away many votes from the DPP. Taking George Chang and Hsu Tien-tsai together, the DPP had won more votes than the two KMT candidates in Tainan city.

The situation in Chiayi city was unique. Chang Po-ya is a close relative of the former city mayor, and her family has ruled the city since 1985.[83] These family relationships make Chiayi city different from other counties and cities. With 50.23 percent of votes the independent candidate Chang Po-ya was way ahead of the KMT and DPP candidates. Chang had emphasized social welfare policy for the elderly, women, laborers, farmers and the handicapped, but she had not promoted old-age allowances like her predecessor. This is because the former city mayor had had to discontinue the old-age allowance after only four months. Although the two opponents of the KMT and the DPP promoted the old-age allowance again, they failed to win the election and even to break Chang Po-ya's absolute majority. The popularity of her family did not leave the other candidates which much chance of election victory.

In Hsinchu county, there was no problem with old-age allowances. The local government paid out TWD 5,000 to all citizens over 65 years. In Ilan county, the old-age benefit had had to be reduced to TWD 3,000 and could only be paid four months a year. In these two counties the continuation of the old-age allowance scheme was of high priority for the electorate and the candidates. In Ilan county, all the candidates were in favor of continuing the old-age allowance system. In Hsinchu county, the elected DPP candidate (Lin Kwang-hua) and the independent candidate (Qiu Ching-chun) – who as third candidate polled over 30 percent of votes – both promoted old-age allowances unlike their opponents.

In Keelung city, Taitung county and Penghu county all candidates promised old-age allowances, as also did the KMT and DPP candidates in Pingtung county. In Changhua there was a neck-and-neck race between the KMT and DPP candidates who both advocated the need for a proper social policy. In Miaoli county, Fu Xue-peng was the only one to support the introduction of an old-age allowance scheme, and he won with a remarkable 54.79 percent of votes. The other candidates did not address the need for better social welfare.

We may conclude that party manifestos in Taipei county started a chain reaction throughout the island. The case studies above confirm the importance of old-age allowances in these counties and cities in the November 29 elections in 1997, as most of the successful candidates had relied on the issue of old-age benefits and social welfare in general. The major conclusion that can be drawn from these case studies is that the topic of social welfare and the resulting election promises are the outcome of intense competition between the candidates. Also, it can be concluded that once social policies have been introduced and the electorate has grown accustomed to having them, they became crucial to winning elections. In the remaining constituencies, the factor social welfare may not have been one of the major election topics.

The DPP had failed to introduce a sustainable old-age allowance system earlier, due to a lack of financial support from the central and provincial governments. The allowance schemes were also hindered by the lack of commitment within the party, as large factions of the DPP, whilst supporting social welfare in general, ruled out the possibility of raising taxes, especially business tax. It should be noted that the small and medium-sized business community supports the DPP much more strongly than it does the KMT. In Taipei county, for example, the DPP won victories in election districts where large industrial areas are dominated by small and medium-sized enterprises, i.e. Sanchung and Hsinchuang. The KMT won in residential areas such as Yunghe and Chunghe rather than in the industrial ones.

In the case of Taipei county,[84] the KMT was particularly successful where the share of the elderly in the population and the electorate is significantly higher. The DPP won in Sanchung, Panchiao and Hsinchuang where the voting population is younger. The age structure of the two major parties provided the occasion and not the reason per se for the promotion of old-age benefits.

The reason for the introduction of the issue of old- age allowances lies in increased competition among the parties. The former unchallenged majority of the KMT was now endangered for the first time by the upcoming DPP. The KMT tried actively to reinforce the issue of old-age allowances in Taipei county. A chain reaction took place, and the KMT candidates in most other counties and cities had to back the proposal of Hsieh Shen-shan. The DPP had no option but to jump on the bandwagon as competition forced each party to match, and possibly outdo, the promises of their political rival. Therefore, party competition in democratic elections can be seen as the key factor in the extension of welfare systems.

Other Changes in Social Welfare Policy

In the context of the impact of electoral party competition on social welfare, it should be noted that the KMT is steadily trying to improve overall social welfare (or at least the legitimization of its government). In November 1997, the cabinet tentatively decided to add four more ministries in the future; the KMT proposed the set up of separate ministries for agriculture, labor, health and welfare, and culture, taking the number of ministries from 8 to 12. The Ministry of Labor would replace the Council of Labor Affairs. The Ministry of Health and Welfare would be reorganized from the Department of Health and the existing social welfare administration will be placed under the Ministry of the Interior.[85] However, these had been long-term plans, which did not materialize over the next years of KMT rule.

The last amendment to the Labor Insurance Act (LIA) improved the qualifying conditions for old-age benefits. On November 6, the council of labor affairs introduced new conditions for drawing old-age benefit in accordance with the new old-age benefit regulation draft. The new conditions are: first, the individual must have worked for more than 15 years and be over 50 years of age, or second, he or she must have worked for more than 20 years. The old conditions (LIA, art. 58) were: more than 15 years work and over 55 years of age or 25 years work. Every employee who had paid in at least for one year and was 60 years old was also entitled to old-age benefit (e.g., in the case of one year just one month's salary).[86] The single benefit paid out amounts to one month's average salary for each of the workers' coverage years. If coverage exceeded 15 years, those years in excess are counted double. The maximum number of months that could be claimed is 45, and 50 if the worker continued to work for five years after reaching the age of 60 (article 59, LIA).[87]

Conclusions

Increased party competition in democratic elections directly promotes the establishment and the extension of social welfare systems. From the global perspective, the spread of democracy and the increase of party competition throughout Asia clearly contribute to improved forms of welfare systems. In 1997, the topic of social welfare, especially with respective to the elderly, was of major importance to the KMT because their electorate was significantly older than that of the DPP – at least in Taipei county, the largest constituency by far. But the age structure alone did not prompt the KMT to focus on old-age allowances. The most important motive for the promotion of social welfare by the KMT was the desire to win the elections. It is for this reason that the old-age allowance scheme (i.e., TWD 5,000 for everyone over 65) constituted a key issue in the November 1997 elections.

Initially, the DPP had wanted to ignore the topic of old-age benefits because the party had to a large extent broken its previous election promises in this regard. However, Hsieh Shen-shan's and Lee Teng-hui's election campaign focused on the issue of old-age allowances and triggered an avalanche of similar proposals from the KMT, the DPP, and many independent candidates. Most other KMT candidates also had to promise social welfare for the elderly, because the people outside of Taipei county did not want to be treated as 'second class citizens'. The DPP quickly returned to the topic of old-age allowances that had been raised by the DPP four years previously in the last local elections owing to increased party competition. In November 1997, the topic of old-age allowances was, thus, again intensively promoted by 42 out of 80 candidates. The majority of candidates focused on social welfare simply in order to win the elections. The example of these 1997 local elections in Taiwan shows that political parties launch new social welfare programs for the purpose of winning elections, and not out of ideological conviction.

6 The Impact of the 1998 Elections on Social Policy

The Taipei and Kaohsiung City Mayor and City Council Elections in 1998

The December 5 elections in 1998 included an election for the Lower House of the Parliament, the Legislative Yuan, and mayoral and city council elections for the two major cities in Taiwan, Taipei and Kaohsiung. Local government elections in other counties and cities had been held the preceding year. During these elections the issue of social welfare was discussed by using the metaphor beef. The issue of beef was talked about in television debates and decorated newspaper headlines.[88] The issue of social welfare, especially the issue of old-age allowances, skyrocketed during the campaigns for the county commissioner and mayoral elections on November 29, 1997. In that year the issue of social welfare for the elderly was put forward by the KMT, but not by the DPP who failed to implement old-age allowances on county and city level in the preceding election period. This was due to lack of support from the Taiwanese central and provincial governments, and fierce opposition in city councils, which were all dominated by the KMT.

The issue of social welfare continued to play an important role in the December 5, 1998 elections. Whereas the issue of social welfare began in the 1997 elections in the northern Taipei county, it was in the southern metropolis of Kaohsiung that the fight for better social welfare policies really took off this time. The strong KMT mayoral candidate in Kaohsiung City, Wu Den-yi, had launched a new social policy program four weeks before polling day, but he still lost to Hsieh Chang-ting, his DPP rival and long-term promoter of social welfare. Social policy was certainly a means of success in the 1998 Kaohsiung mayoral election. In Taipei, mayoral candidates did address the issue of social welfare, but the outcome of the elections was determined more by the voting behavior of New Party followers, who backed mayoral candidate, Ma Ying-jiou, rather than differences in the social welfare policies of the three candidates, Ma Ying-jiou (KMT), Chen Shui-bian (DDP), and Wang Jian-xuan (New Party).

This essay concerns both an analysis of the election results of the 1998 parliamentary elections, and a discussion of the social welfare programs of the candidates and the importance of the issue of social welfare in the high profile mayoral elections that were held at the same time. At the end of this chapter, the results of a content analysis of 397 election programs of candidates in the parliamentary election will be considered, with the contention that this proves that party competition is a driving force behind welfare state construction in Taiwan.

The Evening of Polling Day

In the early evening of polling day many observers spoke of one big winner and two big losers in the elections. However, the later the hour the more it became obvious that the two major opposition parties, which had seemed to be losing just a few hours before, had not actually done too badly.

The DPP lost the mayorship in Taipei county but, in the south of the island, the performance of the DPP Kaohsiung mayoral candidate, Hsieh Chang-ting, surprised not only the ruling KMT but also most DPP members. Until the last few ballot boxes it was not clear who was winning in the Kaohsiung mayoral race. Finally, Hsieh Chang-ting was the lucky winner only 4,565 votes ahead of Wu Den-yi who, like most observers, was surprised by his defeat.

The second surprise in the late evening of polling day was the result of the New Party in the parliamentary elections. Astonishingly, it won four direct parliamentary seats in Taipei alone where the election results came in last. In the two electoral districts in Taipei, the New Party won 18.44 and 16.1 percent of votes.[89] The capital Taipei constitutes a stronghold of the New Party because there is a large Mainland Chinese population. The New Party was once more (i.e. the last time) successful in securing its role as the third force in Taiwanese politics, after heavy losses in the 1997 local elections.

The Results of the City Mayor and City Council Elections

In Taipei City, it was surprising that the then incumbent mayor, Chen Shui-bian, was not reelected, receiving only 45.91 percent of votes. Ma Ying-jiou, mayoral candidate of the KMT, had a landslide victory with 51.13 percent of popular votes. The New Party candidate Wang Jian-xuan only received 2.97 percent of the votes.[90] Nobody could have anticipated exactly how many New Party voters would switch to the Ma Ying-jiou camp. But, it should have been obvious that the situation in 1998 was very different to 1994. Then, there had been a weak KMT candidate and a very strong New Party candidate, thus there was a realistic chance for the latter to be elected. This time the KMT sent one of the most popular KMT politicians, former justice minister Ma Ying-jiou, who also represented an ideal candidate for the New Party electorate. Ma found himself in permanent conflict with Lee Teng-hui, who was heavily opposed by the New Party (which was formed by a former KMT faction). Moreover, Ma had a very strong Mainlander perspective where re-unification was concerned, as he himself was born in Hong Kong. This made Ma Ying-jiou very popular with the Mainland Chinese New Party electorate. The New Party supporters prevented the victory of Mayor Chen Shui-bian (a native Taiwanese) and voted for the KMT candidate. Chen's performance was strong, but the new voting alliance of KMT and New Party supporters in Taipei City could not be rivaled.

As to the Taipei city council elections, it can be seen that the results of the two major parties, KMT and the DPP, resembled to a large extent the results of the city mayoral elections. However, the results for the New Party in the city council elections were much better than in the city mayor election, because many New Party supporters who voted for the KMT mayoral candidate chose a New Party candidate in the city council elections. They did not waste their votes on the likely third position of their own New Party mayoral candidate.

In the Taipei City council election, the New Party won 18.7 percent of the votes and 9 out of 52 seats, the KMT 40.37 percent and 23 seats; and the DPP 31.18 percent and 19 seats. Although all independent candidates together won 6.32 percent of the votes, only one got elected. The votes for the smaller parties: the Green Party, the New Nation Alliance, the Taiwan Independence Party and the China Women's Party only added up to 4.08 percent of votes.[91] The Green Party and the New Nation Alliance and the Taiwan Independence Party, all formed by former DPP members, took away votes from the DPP (and, thus, hindered a better DPP result!). Thus, the KMT and the New Party together retained the majority of seats in the Taipei city council.

Had Chen Shui-bian won again, he would have faced the same situation as in the previous four years, i.e. the united front of KMT and New Party city council members blocking most policy initiatives of the DPP city government. The city council vote against the old-age allowance stipend, which had been paid out for seven months in Taipei city[92] in 1995 was the example par excellence of the strategy of the two former opposition parties in the four preceding years. Whether or not the KMT and the NP had similar policy objectives to the DPP, city council members of both parties tried to obstruct most policy initiatives of the DPP, simply because they came from the DPP.

In Kaohsiung, most people predicted a strong performance by the DPP mayoral candidate, Hsieh Chang-ting. But a victory was only expected by the keenest supporters of the DPP. Like the DPP in Taipei, the KMT thought that their candidate would have quite an easy run in this election. Those who expected a clear victory by the incumbent KMT mayor, Wu Den-yih, witnessed a head to headrace between Hsieh Chang-ting and Wu Den-yih on the evening of polling day. In the end, Hsieh won by the small margin of 0.56 percent, with 48.7 percent of votes.

As to the Kaohsiung mayoral elections, the New Party supporters behaved like their Taipei pendants, i.e. they switched to the side of the KMT. The vast difference between votes for the New Party in the parliamentary election, i.e. 59,930, and the mayoral election, i.e. 6,457, in Kaohsiung disclosed the voting behavior of New Party supporters. While voting for their own party in the parliamentary elections, they preferred to vote for the KMT in the mayoral election. The First-Past-the-Post (i.e. majoritarian) election system used in the mayoral elections influenced voting behavior a great deal.

There are basically two major factors behind the success of Hsieh Chang-ting: his numerous social welfare efforts and the negative campaign of the KMT against Hsieh Chang-ting. Although Wu Den-yih finally turned his attention to existing social problems and introduced a number of new social welfare policies just before the election,[93] he could not shake off the anti-social welfare image he had gained over the past years. Wu could not offer any excuse as to why he had not implemented new social welfare policies in his 8 years of rule in Kaohsiung. Hsieh Chang-tings social welfare program was much more generous than that of his KMT rival.

In the Kaohsiung city council elections, the DPP received 26.81 percent of votes but only 9 out of 44 seats. The KMT secured 45.18 percent of votes and won 25 seats.[94] The New Party followers, who voted for their own party candidates, accounted for 3.84 percent of votes: one seat. The votes for independent candidates added up to 22.3 percent of total votes and secured nine seats, i.e. 20.45 percent of all seats. The only small party that joined the Kaohsiung city council elections, the TAIP, won no seat and had just 1.86 percent of votes.

We see that the New Party achieved quite different results on different levels of the elections. In the two Kaohsiung electoral districts the New Party won many more votes, i.e. 9.83 and 4.79 percent in the parliamentary elections, than in the Kaohsiung mayoral and city council elections.

Furthermore, it needs to be emphasized that one major reason for the vast difference between the output of seats of the KMT and other parties in city council elections lay in the strong local network of the KMT. In addition, the KMT spent a lot of money on bribes and threatened local district chiefs by the use of the local mafia in order to secure a higher voter turnout for the KMT. Another determinant for the comparatively low number of seats won by the DPP and the New Party were the relatively lower numbers of local candidates who are famous public figures.

The Issue of Social Welfare in the City Mayoral Elections

In the 1998 elections, it was KMT mayoral candidate for Kaohsiung city, Wu Den-yih, who first brought up the subject of social welfare. During the 1997 county commissioner and city mayor elections, Wu stated that there was no need to address welfare policies because he had not proposed them in 1994 and had still been elected. President and KMT party chairman Lee Teng-hui, predicted a loss in the 1998 Kaohsiung mayoral elections if Wu would not introduce new social welfare policies.[95] The powerful position and the arguments of Lee Teng-hui convinced Wu Den-yi. In the 1998 mayoral election, Wu put forward a significant package of social welfare policies for the first time.[96] As a consequence of increased pressure coming from the DPP, the then incumbent mayoral candidate of the KMT, Wu Den-yi, launched his new social welfare program in the morning of November 8, 1998. As long as the majority in the mayoral election seemed could be taken for granted, Wu and other KMT incumbents, who were in the same situation, were not willing to promote social policy as the business community, the major sponsor of the costly elections, feared a rise in taxes.

Bearing in mind the attitude Wu expressed in 1997, it is clear that his reason for promoting the issue of social welfare in the 1998 elections was to win the election, not because of his ideology or that of the KMT, and not because of the need of the Kaohsiung people. Of course, the new social policies addressed the needs of Kaohsiung people, however, the needs were not the reason. The needs existed long before. The new social welfare proposals of Wu were: a universal health assistance scheme of TWD 10,000 a year for every Kaohsiung citizen over 65 years of age and the mentally handicapped; a yearly TWD 1,200 subsidy for every household's water bill; free insurance worth TWD 1 million for breast and womb cancer for every female citizen; and two years maternity leave for city government employees with full income maintenance.[97]

The major opponent of Wu Den-yih, Hsieh Chang-ting, proposed a significantly better welfare program. He put forward an annual pension of TWD 36,000 for every citizen over 65; TWD 3,000 for every household to buy a drinking water filter machine; free insurance for breast and womb cancer worth TWD 2 million; two years maternity leave, even for male city government employees, with full income maintenance.[98] Wu earned the reputation of giving empty promises in the two electoral terms he served as city mayor. Hsieh not only proposed higher allowances/awards and subsidies, but he also had the advantage of greater sincerity in proposing these social policies. Hsieh, a then incumbent DPP legislator (and former DPP candidate for vice-president) had become a national celebrity after he had contributed to the solution of the Chen Chin-shing[99] kidnapping affair.[100]

The KMT's strategy in the Kaohsiung mayoral elections was to attack Hsieh for his support of Chen Chin-shing during this event in November 1997. They distributed videotapes in public schools, which contained negative propaganda against Hsieh Chang-ting. The people of Kaohsiung honored the risk Hsieh Chang-ting had taken,[101] rather than listen to the KMT propaganda. In sum, Hsieh's new popularity, the reverse effects of the KMT propaganda against Hsieh, and last but not least, the higher and more sincere social welfare proposals of Hsieh Chang-ting led the DPP to victory in the Kaohsiung mayoral election.

In Taipei City, the issue of social welfare started on November 9, one day later than in Kaohsiung. There was a series of one to one television debates between the three mayoral candidates held by Formosa Television, which received a lot of public attention. On that Monday, it was Ma Ying-jiou and Wang Jian-xuan's turn. Ma concentrated on problems of unfair and backward city development; the elderly; children; and environmental protection.[102] Wang Jian-xuan criticized the social policy of Chen, as Wang thought it would be better to concentrate financial resources on needy pensioners, and not grant them to every citizen. Children of the elderly should be responsible for their welfare and for those without children the government should secure welfare provision.

Ma Ying-jiou agreed in essence with the children's duty to take care of their elderly parents.[103] The next day Chen Shui-bian emphasized his deep concern for the weak groups in society and promised to establish more day care centers for the elderly; more support for the new married couples, single parent families and children; and free meal delivery services for the elderly who live alone.[104]

The major controversy on the third day was the issue of uneven and, therefore, unfair development. The issue of city development was also referred to by the 'beef' metaphor. Ma Ying-jiou accused Chen of not solving the problems of the older city districts, such as Wanhua, Tatung and Shilin.[105] Chen hoped that Taipei would become a city with high social welfare standards. He referred to his past achievements, and said that in four more years he could do even more.[106]

Chen did not explicitly list all his plans for the promotion of social welfare in his most important television debates. His social welfare efforts included, for example, the introduction of old-age allowances in Taipei following the 1994 election. In 1997, Chen again tried to implement an allowance for the disabled elderly. Chen also introduced other new social welfare measures for the elderly during his term.[107] While Chen had the evidence of a record of welfare policies, Wang and Ma could only have referred to the abolition of the old-age allowance, seven months after its implementation, which was conducted by their own fellow party members in the Taipei city council. Ma did not propose any particular welfare measures; he worked with images rather than proposals. He said he would support target groups, but he did not put forward any concrete social policies.[108]

To conclude, the victory of the KMT candidate Ma Ying-jiou rested on the strategic voting behavior of the New Party electorate for whom Ma was an ideal candidate. The shining image of Ma promoted by his election managers helped him to conquer the hearts of many middle class voters, the office people.

The Results and Analyses of the 1998 Parliamentary Elections

The KMT received 46.43 percent of votes and 54.67 percent of seats. The DPP, with about two thirds of the number of nominated candidates of the KMT, won about two thirds of the number of votes of the KMT, i.e. 29.56 percent which meant they won 31.11 percent of the parliamentary seats. The New Party came in third place with 7.06 percent of votes and 4.89 percent of seats.[109] The newly formed Democratic Union (established on June 24, 1998)[110] received an impressive 3.74 percent of votes in their first partici-pation in elections, whereas the earlier established Taiwan Independence Party (established on October 6, 1996) and the Green Party (established on January 25, 1996) only received 1.47 and 0.08 percent respectively.

The New Nation Alliance ranked in fifth place with 1.57 percent of votes, which is a respectable result when considering that it had been founded in September 1998, only a couple of months before the elections. The independent candidates won 9.43 percent of votes and 5.33 percent of seats. Other minor parties, i.e. the China Youth Party, the China Taiwan Aborigine Party, the Nationwide Democratic Non-Partisan Alliance, and the National Democratic Party received only meager shares of votes, i.e. 0.0072, 0.117, 0.658, and 0.0034 percent respectively.[111]

Interpreting the results of Table 40, it can be seen that the Kuomintang did not win significantly more votes, just more seats, compared to the last parliamentary elections. It needs to be said that the KMT won 0.37 percent more votes compared to the 1994 parliamentary elections.[112] The DPP lost 3.61 percent and the New Party lost 5.89 percent, whereas the independent candidates together won 1.699 percent[113] more votes than four years ago.

Table 40: Results of 1998 Parliamentary Elections[114]

Name of party	Percentage of valid votes	Number of directly electable candidates	Number of directly elected candi-dates	Number of election districts with directly electable candidates	Number of aborigine consti-tuencies[115] with directly electable candidates	Number of non-directly elected candidates	Percentage of parliamen-tary seats
China Nationalist Party, KMT	46.4304	115	96	29	2	27	54.67
Democratic Pro-gressive Party, DPP	29.5624	79	52	27	2	18	31.11
New Party, NP	7.0594	36	7	27		4	4.89
Democratic Union, DU	3.7378	21	4	17	1		1.78
New Nation Alliance, NNA	1.5726	12	1	12			0.44
Taiwan Independence Party, TAIP	1.446	17	1	17			0.44
Nat.-wide Dem. Non-part. Alliance, NDNA	0.658	5	3	3	2		1.33
Green Party, GP	0.0806	1		1			-
China Taiwan Abo-rigine Party, CTAP	0.0117	1			1		-
China Youth Party, CYP	0.0072	1		1			-
National Democratic Party, NDP	0.0034	1		1			-
Independent candidates	9.4305	108	12		1		5.33
Total	100	397	176	-	-	49	100

Therefore, we cannot speak of a tremendous shift in voters' preferences. The DPP lost votes due to the foundation of the Green Party, the Taiwan Independence Party and the New Nation Alliance, all of which were formed by former DPP factions. The DPP had to share its former electorate with these parties, whose shares of votes added up to 3.099 percent.

A second factor weakening the result of the DPP (when bearing the good performance in the November 1997 elections in mind) is the increased number of seats available in the Lower House of Parliament, i.e. 225 instead of 164 seats. As the DPP is a relatively new party (founded on September 28, 1986) the number of famous candidates available for candidacy is relatively limited. The SNTV electoral system supports those candidates who are famous. In the SNTV system, voters primarily vote for candidates, not parties. Thus, the relatively small number of well-known candidates contributed to the relative weakness of the DPP when compared to the vast human resources of the KMT. The KMT had no problem filling up their pool of candidates because dozens of very famous KMT members, formerly employed in the Provincial Assembly (which is about to be dissolved) with strong factional support on county level, joined the ranks of KMT candidates in the parliamentary elections.

It is for this major reason that the overwhelming victory of the DPP in the 1997 county commissioner and city mayor elections cannot be directly compared with this years parliamentary election.

As to both 1998 mayoral elections, it can be seen that the DPP did quite well. Chen Shui-bian was able to extend his electorate in the 1998 Taipei city mayoral election, and support for Hsieh Chang-ting in the 1998 Kaohsiung city mayoral election was unexpectedly high. The New Party lost almost half of its former electorate in the 1998 parliamentary election. The internal fighting that damaged the image of the party may constitute the major reason for the New Party's losses. The number of New Party candidates that could have been elected directly increased from 35 to 36.[116] Many New Party voters may have returned to the KMT and/or turned to the Democratic Union which showed a good first time performance with 3.74 percent of votes[117] (the Democratic Union is mainly made up of former KMT members)[118] and/or more popular independent candidates.

The Impact of the Electoral System and Party Competition on the Candidates' Social Welfare Proposals in the Parliamentary Elections

A content analysis of all the election programs of candidates in the 1998 parliamentary election was conducted, in order to investigate the impact of party competition and electoral system[119] on the quantity and quality (i.e.

the form) of individual candidates' and parties' welfare proposals. From the original 398 candidates, whose election programs were distributed to each household just before the elections, one candidate from Hsinchu city canceled her participation in these elections.

The candidates have been categorized along quantitative and qualitative lines. The candidates were first divided into four groups according to their welfare efforts (see Table 2).[120] Category 1 includes those candidates with three or more concrete welfare proposals, such as fighting for the introduction of a national pension scheme or unemployment insurance; changing the premium rate system of the national health insurance; lowering education fees, and the like. Category 2 includes those candidates with one or two concrete welfare proposals. Categories 3 and 4 include those who put forward only vague welfare proposals and no welfare proposal respectively. In Table 41 we see that most candidates range in Category 2, i.e.142 candidates. Category 3 ranks second with 118 candidates. In the highest category there were 38 candidates, and in the lowest category there were 99.

When looking at the candidates' success rate, it can be seen that those candidates with a greater number of concrete welfare proposals were preferred by the electorate to those who made fewer; vague; or no concrete promises. These results suggest that the electorate responded to welfare programs, and that candidates made welfare proposals in order to secure a competitive advantage over other candidates.

Table 41: The Distribution of Candidates According to Concrete Welfare Proposals and their Electoral Success

Category of concrete proposals	Number of candidates	Thereof elected	Percentage
1	38	24	63.2
2	142	66	46.5
3	118	53	44.9
4	99	33	33.3
All	397	176	44.3

By focusing on the distribution in these four categories, it is possible to rank the parties according to the quantity and quality of their election promises, in the field of social welfare policies (see Table 42). The average category achieved by candidates of one party is calculated. By proceeding thus, it can be seen that the New Nation Alliance ranks first, in front of the DPP, the Democratic Union, the KMT and the New Party. These are the five strongest parties in these elections.

Table 42: The Distribution of Candidates by Categories (of Welfare Proposals), Party, the Average Category of a Party, and the Ranking of Parties in Proposing Social Welfare

Party	Category 1	Category 2	Category 3	Category 4	Average	Rank
NNA	23.1	61.5	7.7	7.7	2.0	1
DPP	21.5	40.5	19.0	19.0	2.4	2
DU	9.5	42.9	33.3	14.3	2.5	3
KMT	9.6	36.5	36.5	17.4	2.6	4
NP	2.8	27.8	44.4	25.0	2.9	5
CYP	–	–	100.0	–	3.0	6
GP	–	–	100.0	–	3.0	7
Indep.	2.8	34.3	25.9	37.0	3.0	8
NDP	–	–	100.0	–	3.0	9
TAIP	5.9	23.5	23.5	47.1	3.1	10
NDNA	–	20.0	40.0	40.0	3.2	11
CTAP	–	–	–	100.0	4.0	12
Total	9.5	35.9	29.6	24.9	2.7	

The New Nation Alliance and the Democratic Union were formed out of splinter groups of the DPP and the KMT respectively. The results of the other minor parties do not represent a major anti-welfare stand, but rather the small number of candidates or the focus on other important issues, such as in the case of the Taiwan Independence Party. The two liberal parties ranking on top (NNA, DPP) score higher than their two conservative counterparts (DU, KMT). The New Party scored below average.

In Table 43, it can be seen that candidates, who proposed the reform or the introduction of a national social system, were significantly more successful in gaining a seat in the parliament than their counterparts. Those who proposed a national pension scheme were comparably very successful in obtaining a seat in parliament.

Among concrete welfare proposals, the introduction of a national pension scheme was most frequently proposed. This reflects the electorate's concern about the long existing and unsolved problems of the rising needs of the elderly.[121] Before the recent elections, the elderly demonstrated for the introduction of welfare benefits for the elderly, especially old-age allowances.

Table 43: The Most Frequent Concrete Welfare Proposals and their Impact on Voting Behavior

Major social welfare proposals in the public election circulars	Number of candidates	Thereof elected	Percentage
Introduction of pension insurance	85	55	64.7
Reform of health insurance	82	42	51.2
Introduction of unemployment insurance	72	39	54.2
Total	389	176	45.2

Old-age allowances were introduced on county and city level in Taiwan in the 1993 county commissioner and city mayoral elections. The DPP was the first party that proposed the introduction of old-age allowances. The old-age allowance system serves as gap filler until the first pensions are paid out under the national pension scheme.

The second most frequently made welfare proposal was the reform of the national health insurance system,[122] as many citizens were complaining about the unfair premiums; the allocation of financial resources; the additional high registration fees in hospitals; the unfair system of compulsory membership; and equal premium fees with an unequal distribution of health institutions across the country, etc.

The third most mentioned reform proposal was the introduction of a national unemployment insurance system. Unemployment is a relatively new problem in Taiwan. The recent changes in the international economy, especially the expatriation of industries, have increased international competition between national economies for low-wage induced foreign investments. This, and the, then, impending entry of Taiwan into the WTO (World Trade Organization) enhanced the problem of unemployment.

The analysis also included a qualitative comparison of the content of election programs. Here, three categories describing the social policy strategies pursued by each party are used (see Table 44). The first category comprises those candidates who focused on the majority of the electorate (e.g.: the elderly and women; or the elderly, the unemployed, and those facing the possibility of unemployment; or women, and households with school children, etc.). Candidates in the second category proposed welfare programs directed at a minority of the electorate (e.g.: soldiers, the weak, and the handicapped or fishermen, and the elderly without family assistance). Those who did not put forward welfare policies are found in the third category.

The distribution of parties in Table 44 discloses the overall strategies of parties and their candidates with regard to welfare policy. The main findings here are, first, that the majority of candidates (62 percent) pursued a catch-all strategy in their welfare proposals, and, second, that the strategic target groups of welfare proposals matches the structure of the electorate, rather than the needs of the entire population.

The overwhelming majority of candidates of four out of the five largest parties fall into the catch-all category, which represents party support stemming from all major social groups. Only the New Party concentrated on welfare proposals particularly designed for the Mainland Chinese minority. This reflects a specific electorate, which is mainly composed of (veteran) soldiers and officials, and their families.

Table 44: The Welfare Strategy of Candidates per Party

Party	Number of candidates	A catch-all strategy	Focusing on particular groups	No social welfare policies proposed
KMT	115	**71.3%**	10.4%	18.3%
DPP	78	**73.1%**	6.4%	20.5%
NP	36	47.2%	**27.8%**	25.0%
DU	21	**76.2%**	9.5%	14.3%
NNA	13	**84.6%**	7.7%	7.7%
TAIP	17	52.9%	5.9%	**41.2%**
Other parties	9	55.6%	11.1%	33.3%
Indep. candidates	108	**46.3%**	16.7%	37.0%
Total	397	62.2%	12.6%	25.2%

The data of these content analyses show that there is a direct impact of social welfare proposals on electoral outcomes. This conclusion is not surprising, as debates during previous elections and the parallel high-profile Taipei and Kaohsiung city mayor elections also highlighted the importance of social welfare issues.

The main task of this study is to investigate the impact of party competition on social policy. Thus, we need to look into the degree of electoral competition in each constituency and the degree of welfare proposals made, this will now ensue.

Table 45: The Positive Association of Electoral Competition per Constituency (Measured by the GINI Coefficient of Vote Distribution of Candidates) and the Number of Concrete Social Welfare Proposals ($G = 0.625$, $r_S = 0.374$)[123]

Constituency	SW Index	Classified as	GINI coefficient of vote distribution[124]	Classified as
Tainan city	1.54	H	0.277	H
Chiayi city	1.83	H	0.486	L
Ilan county	2.00	H	0.272	H
Tainan county	2.31	H	0.318	H
Kaohsiung county	2.33	H	0.241	H
Chiayi county	2.40	H	0.522	L
Keelung city	2.40	H	0.239	H
Changhua county	2.45	H	0.339	H
Hualien county	2.50	H	0.339	H
Taipei county 3	2.53	M	0.400	M
Miaoli county	2.55	M	0.478	L
Kaohsiung city 1	2.64	M	0.426	M
Kaohsiung city 2	2.64	M	0.454	M
Yunlin county	2.67	M	0.345	H
Pintung county	2.69	M	0.379	M
Taipei county 1	2.70	M	0.459	M
Hsinchu city	2.75	L	0.470	L
Taipei city 2	2.80	L	0.643	L
Taoyuan county	2.88	L	0.392	M
Nantou county	2.91	L	0.339	H
Taichung city	2.95	L	0.476	L
Hsinchu county	3.00	L	0.475	L
Taipei city 1	3.06	L	0.360	M
Taipei county 2	3.08	L	0.481	L
Taichung county	3.18	L	0.364	M

Party competition can be measured by the evenness in the distribution of votes by candidates. In doing so, the distribution of votes is analyzed by using the GINI coefficient. The more evenly the votes are distributed between candidates of one constituency, the higher is the electoral competition in that particular constituency.[125] The degree of candidates' welfare proposals in each constituency is determined by calculating the average category of our four welfare categories (see Table 45).

After correlating the ranks of each constituency in respect of the intensity of party competition and welfare proposals, it can be seen that there is a strong positive relationship between the ranking of the GINI indexes, indicating the degree of party competition, and the ranking, indicating the intensity of social welfare proposals.

The gamma coefficent (G) for the two rankings in concern (see Table 45) is 0.625 and thus demonstrates a strong positive relationship. Spearman's rho is 0.374. This confirms the existence of a positive relationship between party competition and the extent of welfare policy proposals in democratic elections. Out of nine constituencies that rank highest in terms of social welfare proposals, seven also rank highest in terms of party competition. This finding supports the thesis of the author, which identifies party competition in democratic elections as one of the major driving forces behind welfare state formation and development.

Another contention, relating to the policy centered group of welfare theories noted earlier, is that different electoral systems influence social policy outcomes in different ways. As to elections in Taiwan, the relatively unproportional character;[126] the plurality of elections; and the competition-increasing effect of the SNTV system, must be considered:

In every elections district there are a certain number of candidates competing for a limited number of seats. The votes for those candidates who have lost are not transferable, unless they can be won back on national level. This resembles strongly unproportional effects of majoritarian election systems, also called First-Past-The-Post system (FPTP).[127] In Taiwan, 78.2 percent of parliamentarians are elected directly. Only 49 out of 225 parliamentary seats are distributed proportionally. Smaller parties are excluded from the blessing effects of the distribution of national seats (see Table 40).

Every election in a constituency is an independent election. Candidates do not consider overall party strategies and cannot rely solely on the popularity of the party if there is another candidate from the same party in the same constituency (as is the normal case in Taiwan). Candidates' campaigns on the constituency level, and not party campaigns on a national level, determine the election results. Thus, we have hundreds of campaigns by hundreds of candidates, and dozens of separate elections. In other words, in each constituency there is a separate election.

Directly elected candidates face fierce competition from all sides. We see that one practical effect of the SNTV system is to intensify the competition between candidates of the same party,[128] and thus overall party competition. Therefore, the SNTV system strengthens electoral competition, much more than proportional and majoritarian election systems.

Furthermore, we conclude that the degree of party competition varies from one constituency to another because candidates of one constituency only compete with each other, and the number of candidates and especially strong[129] candidates vary across constituencies. Contrary to proportional and majoritarian election systems, the SNTV system is directly responsible for huge differences in electoral competition among candidates of different constituencies (and not the number of competing parties or the regional power structure of parties). The analysis of election programs above reveals that the quantity and quality of concrete welfare proposals varied greatly among different constituencies (Tables 45 and 46).

It can be concluded that different degrees of party competition are responsible for the differences in candidate's welfare proposals between constituencies. Some constituencies such as Tainan city, Chiayi city, Ilan county, Tainan county and Kaohsiung county show both a high degree of party competition and high levels of welfare policies. Taichung county, Taipei county 2, Taipei city 1, and Hsinchu county, on the other hand, show low levels of welfare policies of candidates and medium to low levels of party competition. Thus it may be asserted that the SNTV election system applied in Taiwan is a relatively unproportional election system. It has also been found that the SNTV system has a competitive effect, as it is not the number of national parties joining the election, but the number and the strength of candidates in each constituency, that determines the degree of electoral competition.

In Table 45, only average categories per constituency were calculated, without knowing about the structure of the distribution of the data, for example, the variation. In order to prove the existence of clusters of behavior of candidates (i.e. a high similarity of welfare proposals) in each constituency, the variation of the number of candidates per welfare category must be calculated and compared to the variation of the overall number of candidates per category (see Table 46). The method of the coefficient of variation is applied, because it allows the comparison of variations of constituencies with different numbers of candidates and different means.[130] The smaller the relative variation, the higher is the concentration of our results around the average.

In eleven out of 31 constituencies the coefficient of variation is significantly lower than the overall coefficient of variation, whereas only in two constituencies is there a higher coefficient of variation (see Table 47).

Table 46: Classification of Candidates per Welfare Proposals Made and the Comparison of the Coefficients of Variation Between Constituencies[131]

Constituency	Cat. 1	Cat. 2	Cat. 3	Cat. 4	Index of the Coefficient of Variation[132]	Evaluation[133]
Aborigines Lowland	1	1		4	1.09	similar
Aborigines Highland			3	6	0.37	sign. lower[134]
Changhua county	3	9	4	4	1.13	higher
Chiayi city	2	3	1		1.07	similar
Chiayi county		6	4		0.58	sign. lower
Hsinchu city	1	2	3	2	1.00	same
Hsinchu county		2	2	2	0.78	sign. lower
Hualien county		3	3		0.57	sign. lower
Ilan county	3	1	1	1	1.65	sign. higher
Kaohsiung city 1	1	5	2	3	1.06	similar
Kaohsiung city 2		7	5	2	0.77	sign. lower
Kaohsiung county	3	6	4	2	1.15	higher
Keelung city		3	2		0.58	sign. lower
Kinmen county		2	2	1	0.76	sign. lower
Lianchiang county		1			-	no variation
Miaoli county	1	5	3	2	1.00	same
Nantou county		3	6	2	0.65	sign. lower
Penghu county		2		1	1.01	similar
Pintung county	1	8	2	5	1.04	similar
Taichung city	1	6	6	7	0.89	lower
Taichung county		5	8	9	0.70	sign. lower
Tainan city	6	7			0.92	similar
Tainan county	3	7	4	2	1.13	higher
Taipei city 1		6	5	7	0.79	sign. lower
Taipei city 2	1	10	13	6	0.81	lower
Taipei county 1	2	8	8	5	0.96	similar
Taipei county 2	1	7	6	11	0.86	lower
Taipei county 3	5	4	5	5	1.29	sign. higher
Taitung county		3	1		0.55	sign. lower
Taoyuan county	2	5	13	6	0.84	lower
Yunlin county	1	5	3	3	1.01	similar
Total	38	142	119	98	1.00	

This result demonstrates that – owing to the specific feature of the SNTV system – the variation of the distribution of proposed welfare policies tends to be lower on constituency level than nationwide. This means that the strength (regarding quantity and quality) of welfare proposals cluster in each constituency.

This implies that candidates tend to promise as much as their competitors do, and that candidates tend not to focus on social welfare policies when nobody else does. The more candidates of one constituency promise to implement social policies, the more everybody else will put forward social welfare policies. Owing to the very nature of the SNTV election system social policy proposals tend to resemble each other in each constituency.

It is noted that, because of the SNTV election system, there is a higher degree of party competition; and, also, a relationship between welfare promises within each constituency.

Table 47: Comparison of the Variation of the Number of Candidates per Welfare Category of Each Constituency and the Variation of all Candidates, in Number of Constituencies[135]

Higher	3	Same	2
Sign. higher	**2**	Similar	8
Lower	4	No variation	1
Sign. lower	**11**	Total	31

In the 1998 elections for the Taiwanese Lower House of the Parliament there were 397 candidates in 31 constituencies. The number of equally strong candidates in each constituency directly influences the degree of party competition. However, the number of political parties and their relative strength is not relevant to the degree of electoral competition in SNTV elections.

All in all, it can be concluded that the SNTV system causes different degrees of competition in each constituency, and that different degrees of party competition cause different degrees of electoral promises in the field of social welfare. Social policy is, thus, not only determined by the conduct of democratic elections but also by the degree of party competition, which is, in turn, determined to a large extent by the electoral system in use.

Conclusion

The empirical results of the content analysis of 397 election programs has shown that electoral competition is the main determinant in the number and extent of welfare proposals made by candidates in democratic elections. Electoral competition varies due to the specific features of electoral systems and party systems. Since the (gradual) introduction of democracy beginning in 1987, Taiwan's political system has undergone manifold changes. A thoroughly democratic regime has replaced the former authoritarian martial law regime of the KMT. In the 1990s, Taiwan had developed a multi-party system with two dominating parties.

In the 1997 county commissioner and city mayor elections the DPP received, for the first time, more absolute votes and many more offices than the long term ruling KMT. Though having experienced a setback in the 1998 parliamentary elections (owing to a couple of factions breaking away from the DPP), the DPP proved that it was able to become the strongest political party countrywide.

To conclude, party competition does not start with equal shares of votes in parliamentary elections but much earlier, with the upcoming thread of an advancing opposition party. Certainly, the strong performance of the DPP in the last elections (and not the need for social welfare as proposed by functionalist welfare theories) put pressure on the KMT and forced it to introduce one social reform after the other. The development of party competition in the recent Taiwanese election strongly resembles that of Germany in the first two decades after World War II, where the long-term ruling Conservative government was put under increasing pressure by the major opposition party.[136]

The major changes in the Taiwanese social system implemented since the mid-1990s, were the result of increased party competition in democratic elections. The planned introduction of a national pension and realized unemployment insurance benefit of the Labor Insurance (implemented in 1998) were also the outcome of intensified electoral competition in the later half of the 1990s. The particular type of election system applied in Taiwan, the SNTV system, increases overall electoral competition, especially also between candidates of the same party. The Taiwanese example demonstrates the great potential of democratic competition among parties and candidates as a driving force behind welfare state construction in East Asia.

7 Conclusions

Taiwan represents not an exception in East Asian welfare state development since conservative political parties conduct unmistakably conservative social policy. The Kuomintang never envisioned the establishment of generous welfare state programs, which would have endangered the financial means that were necessary for war efforts on the mainland (with the Japanese and the communists) and defense efforts after its retreat to Taiwan. Moreover, the Kuomintang represented the interests of major industrialists who, of course, shied the implementation of either contributory social insurance schemes, that are largely paid by employers and employees, or non-contributory social assistance schemes, that are financed by taxes, of which the vast majority derives from land and business taxes in Taiwan. Taiwanese authorities, hence, prefer that the market plays a major role in welfare provision, and are highly reluctant to allow an increase in welfare and social security programs that involve a financial commitment of the state.

The Taiwanese welfare state system features low levels of governmental welfare expenditures in comparison to the Western world, a strong role of the market and the family in welfare provision, and a strong role of the state as a regulator in welfare provision. But, the Taiwanese welfare state system is expanding quickly with regard to the number of new social insurance and social assistance schemes and with regard to the coverage of existing schemes. The new development in Taiwanese social politics has nothing to do with a more or less profound change of attitudes of the governing elites. The ruling parties, and the majority of the people, still adhere to conservative social policy doctrinces, such as a rejection of dependency-creating welfare programs, a strong emphasis of the responsibility of the family and the individuals in taking care of themselves, and a dislike of state wefare programs (see Table 48).

Recent efforts in the field of social policy are to be seen as the direct outcome of the process of democratization. High party competition and the emergence of numerous social welfare movements, such as the handicapped welfare movement, the elderly welfare movement, the women's welfare movement, the child welfare movement, and many more, have forced politicians and political parties to change their policy objectives in social policy as a whole.

Table 48: Features of Conservative Social Policy in Taiwan

Criteria	Features of Conservative Social Policy in Taiwan
Market-State relations in welfare provision	Before: Except for state provision aimed at special interest groups, the market and the family stood in the center of welfare provision. Now: Both market and state welfare provision are emphasized.
Government's attitude towards welfare dependency	The government opposes welfare dependency.
Government's attitude towards redistributive welfare programs	The government opposes redistributive welfare programs.
Government's attitude towards government spending on social welfare	Both KMT and DPP, in essence, oppose government spending on social welfare, but big exceptions are made in times of local and national elections.
Type of social insurance schemes preferred	Occupational insurance schemes for pensions (only partly implemented); Universal insurance scheme for health care.
Main target groups for welfare state institutions	Formerly: military servants and government employees. Now: the masses of people.
Welfare ideology promoted by government	Government promotes mainly conservative welfare ideologies focusing on individual responsibility for welfare provisions.
Major reasons for welfare state extensions	1. High party competition in democratic elections. 2. A large number of strong social welfare movements. 3. Demographic and societal changes: especially aging of society, rise of nuclear family pattern, and increased female labor force participation.

While demographic and societal changes, such as the aging of the population, the rise of nuclear families, and higher labor force participation of women, multiplied overall welfare needs of society, this rise in demands would not have been a sufficient condition for the rise of welfare policy since the late 1980s; but only an additional necessary condition.

The policy directives changed from providing a social safety net for privileged groups only to addressing the social needs of the mass of people, as well as a greater number of needy groups of society. The principally highly conservative policy stand in welfare politics was altered and a new moderate conservative social policy came into being. This new policy constitutes a compromise between ideological rejections of costly welfare policies – be they non-funded or partly funded social insurance or social assistance programs – and the political necessity of granting concessions to powerful segments of the electorate. As a result, the new conservative social policy paradigm becomes visible in the implementation and extension of universal social policy schemes while fiscal constraints due to conservative policy stands are retained.

The new mix of occupationally divided and new universal social policy measures, especially the National Health Insurance and the locally implemented old-age allowances, have led to a change in the course of welfare state development in Taiwan, which now forms together with South Korea a sub-group in the rim of East Asian welfare states that is based on universal health care and occupationally divided pension systems. In case, the universal locally granted old-age allowance payments lead to the creation of a non-contributory universal pension system, or a two-tier pension system with a universal pension scheme based on citizenship and a second-tier contributory, supplementary pension scheme (such as in Sweden), Taiwan would surpass even moderate conservative social politics of e.g. Italy – in terms of its universal features – which also applies a mix of universal health care and with occupational pension systems.

Notes

1 Also referred to as Taiwanese.
2 The name of these amendments has been changed to Temporary Provisions Effective During the Period of Communist Rebellion in 1960 (TP, 1960).
3 For further details on the land reform see: Chen Cheng (1961), *Land Reform in Taiwan*, China Publishing, Taipei, 1961; and Fei, John C.H., Ranis, Gustav and Kuo, Shirley W.Y. (1979), *Growth With Equity: The Taiwan Case*, Oxford University Press: New York, 1979.
4 The date (that is referring to the *Er-Er-Ba Incident* on February 28, 1947) is a clear sign for the aim of the killings, i.e. to destroy the moral of opposition leaders by killing their family members; for further details of this incident please also see Bruce Jacobs (2000), Completing the Circle, *Taipei Times*, March 23.
5 The two largest cities, Taipei and Kaohsiung, voted one year later in 1998 when the DPP lost the mayorship of Taipei to the KMT, and the KMT lost that of Kaoshiung to the DPP.
6 The eight counties won by the KMT were: Changhua county, Yunlin county, Chiayi county, Hualien county, Taitung county, Penghu county, Kinmen county, and Lianchiang county.
7 i.e. between the end of the Temporary Provisions on May 31, 1991, and the Constitutional amendment of May/July 1997.
8 This refers to land only, not houses built, trees planted, embankments and drains (ibid.: 180).
9 The Additional Article 18(3) of 1992 has been designated Additional Article 10(4) in the constitutional amendment of 1997.
10 The interpretation for the election regulation provided by Art. 26 of the Constitution were to be interpreted by the Council of Grand Justices whose judicial decisions have – for four decades – set off the election for the National Assembly.
11 Which incorporated the revolutionary Nationalist forces in Mainland China that have been united in the *Tung Meng Hui* since 1905 in Tokyo into a political party that aimed to unify China and transform it from being a backward, suppressed country into a powerful, fully independent country.
12 Important constitutional reforms have been conducted in 1948 (TP), 1966 (TP), 1991, 1992, 1994, 1997, and 1999.
13 The most important reforms of the state were conducted in 1950-52; in 1972 and the following years; in 1993, with the end of military influence on the Executive Yuan (Tien, 1996: 3; Dickson, 1996: 50); in 1994, reform of Constitution for direct elections of President; in 1997, reform of Constitution for the suspension of Provincial Assembly elections, in 1999, the reform of the National Assembly elections and its powers.
14 During the time of martial law the KMT had two faces one that of the promoter of liberalization and democratization, social welfare policies (see the Principle of Livelihood); and one that of the KMT 'White Terror' that killed thousands of opposition activists as well as their family members.

15 The change of the KMT towards realizing the fact that Communist China had won the Civil War; that the territory of the Republic of China does not comprehend all of China; and that the Republic of China on Taiwan has been a de facto independent country that has been separated from Mainland China since 1949.
16 In the 1990s, the Hakka supported was divided equally between the KMT (whose former chairman, Lee Teng-hui, belongs to the ethnic group of Hakka) and the DPP (which also featured prominent Hakka politicians, such as Hsu Hsin-liang).
17 Kaohsiung county shares comprises both Metropolitan suburbs of Kaohsiung and a rather huge stretch of land located away from the coastal area.
18 The statements varied: PM Hsiao on Nov. 2 said TWD 7,000 to 8,000 (in *Zhong Yang Ri Bao News*); CEPD on Nov. 6 said TWD 6,000 (in *Zi You Ri Bao*); Lee Gau-chao (CEPD vice-chairman) on Nov. 7 said TWD 7,000 to 8,500 (in *Zi You Ri Bao*).
19 Cf *Zhong Yang Ri Bao*, Nov. 2, *Min Zhong Shi Wan Bao* Nov. 2, 1997; and *Zi You Ri Bao*, Nov. 6 and 7, 1997.
20 Cf *Zhong Yang Ri Bao*, Nov. 2, *Min Zhong Shi Wan Bao*, Nov. 2, 1997; and *Zi You Ri Bao*, Nov. 7, 1997.
21 'Islandwide' with the exception of the Kaoshiung and Taipei city mayor elections of 1994 (last elections were won by the DPP in Taipei and the KMT in Kaoshiung in 1994).
22 Cf *The China Post*, Nov. 28, 1997.
23 Cf *United Daily*, Nov. 30, 1997, p. 2.
24 Cf *Tai Wan Ri Bao*, Nov. 30, 1997, p. 6.
25 Cf ibid, p. 1.
26 Cf for example Political Science Professor Chu Yun-han, an expert who gave his comments on the Nov. 29 elections said – falsely – that the KMT might lose its legislative majority in the 1998 elections; cf *The China Post*, Dec. 1, 1997.
27 Cf *China News*, Nov. 8, 1997, p. 6.
28 Cf *China News*, Nov. 15, 1997.
29 Cf *Tai Wan Shi Bao*, Nov. 30, 1997.
30 Cf *Min Zhong Shi Wan Bao*, Nov. 30, 1997; and Lindy Yeh, *Taipei Times*, Dec. 2, 2001.
31 This equals roughly USD 160.
32 In Tapei city, Aborigines and handicapped people could receive old-age allowances already from the age of 55, cf Sun, 1997, p. 82.
33 Interview with Liu Tao, DPP headquarters, Taipei, Nov. 97.
34 Cf ibid.
35 For example, the distribution of local taxes in Taipei city in 1995 was: 62.78% Business Tax, 17.4% Land Value Increase Tax, and 7.82% Land Tax; cf Taipei Municipal Government (1997), *The Statistical Abstract of Taipei Municipality*, pp. 236-7.
36 The KMT and the New Party together held the majority in the city council and therefore blocked the allowance payments to the elderly.
37 Cf *The China Post*, Nov. 1, 1997.
38 Cf *Min Zhong Shi Wan Bao*, Nov. 2, 1997.
39 Cf *The China Post*, Nov. 7, 1997.
40 Cf *Zi You Ri Bao*, Nov. 7, 1997.
41 Cf *Zi You Ri Bao*, Nov. 1, 1997.
42 Cf *Zi You Ri Bao*, Nov. 1, 1997.
43 Cf *Zi You Ri Bao*, Nov. 7, 1997.
44 Cf *Zhong Yang Ri Bao*, Nov. 2, 1997.
45 Cf *Zi You Ri Bao*, Nov. 2, 1997.

46 Cf *China News*, Nov. 4, 1997.
47 Cf *Zi You Ri Bao*, Nov. 7, 1997.
48 Taipei and Kaoshiung cities elect their mayors one year after the other parts of Taiwan.
49 Cf *Zi You Ri Bao*, Nov. 7, 1997.
50 Cf ibid.
51 Cf *Min Zhong Shi Wan Bao*, Nov. 24, 1997.
52 Cf *Zi You Ri Bao*, Nov. 7, 1997.
53 Cf *The China Post*, Nov. 1, 1997.
54 Cf '*Gong Bao*' of each county/city for the Nov. 29 elections 1997 available at the election commission of the Taiwan provincial government.
55 Cf refers to statements such as 'take care of the elderly' or 'promote social welfare' or stating exclusively welfare for a special group such as the handicapped only.
56 Cf refers to candidates who did not mention social welfare policies as major topics at all, but still conducted one or the other kind of minor social policies. cf the candidates' policies in the '*Gong Bao*'.
57 He proposed to hold a referendum against the establishment of a chemical factory by the German Bayer group. His smaller welfare policies are, for example, shelters for physically abused women and welfare for the handicapped; cf *China News*, Nov. 27, 1997.
58 Cf Liao Feng-chen (1997), 'Nian Jin Huan Xuan Piao, You Piao?', *Global Views Monthly*, No. 11, p. 172.
59 Cf *Tai Wan Shi Bao*, Nov. 30, 1997, p. 6.
60 Cf *China News*, Nov. 26, 1997, p. 12.
61 Cf calculated from *United Daily*, Nov. 30, 1997; not included are the outer island counties, Kinmen and Lienchiang, constituencies which are too small to be considered here; Taipei city and Kaoshiung city elect their mayors separately one year after the other constituencies.
62 There was a by-election in March 1997 following the murder of the KMT county commissioner.
63 1997 the share of KMT votes has been calculated from two candidates nominated by the KMT.
64 Two candidates nominated by the KMT in 1997.
65 Cf *Zi You Ri Bao*, Nov. 30, 1997, p. 6; *Zi Li Cao Bao*, Nov. 30, 1997, p. 3; *Tai Wan Ri Bao*, Nov. 30, 1997, p. 3; *China News*, Nov. 30, 1997, p. 3, and *TVBS Zhou Kan*, 6. Dec. 1997, cover story.
66 Cf *China News*, ibid.
67 Cf *Tai Wan Shi Bao*, Nov. 30, 1997, p. 23.
68 Cf poll by *TVBS Zhou Kan*, Nov. 22, 1997, p. 46 (N=1108, for 9-10. Nov.); and *TVBS Zhou Kan*; and poll by *Zhong Shi Wan Bao*, Nov. 25 to 27, 1997 (25.11.: 5,300 votes for each, i.e., Su and Hsieh, and 27.11.: 6,800 votes each).
69 DGBAS (1996), *Social Indicators*, pp. 292-5; and the *Zi Li Cao Bao*, Nov. 30 1997, p. 17; the candidates were: Hsieh Shen-shan (KMT), Su Zhen-chang (DPP), Lin Chih-chia (ex-KMT, independent), Liao Xue-guang (ex-DPP, independent), Yang Tai-shuen (New Party), and Angela Zhou (ex-New Party, independent).
70 The average share of people over 65 (in the population) in this sample is 6%, therefore the following classification was made: under 4% = 'lowest', 4.1 to 5.0% = 'very low', 5.1 to 5.5% = 'low', 5.6 to 6.4% = 'normal', 6.5 to 7.0% = 'high', 7.1 to 8.0% = 'very high', over 8% = 'highest'. The intervals for 'low' and 'high' had been chosen smaller in order to be more sensitive as they are next to the category 'normal'.
71 This is the translation used in government publications.

72 Interview with Liu Tao, DPP headquarters, Nov. 1997.
73 Calculated from DGBAS, Social Indicators; and *Zi Li Cao Bao*, Nov. 30, 1997, p. 17; vote-index = votes for Su Zhen-chang (DPP) / votes for Hsieh Shen-shan (KMT).
74 Cf DGBAS (1996), *Social Indicators*, pp. 292 ff.
75 Cf *Tai Wan Ri Bao*, Nov. 30, 1997, p. 22.
76 Cf *China News*, Nov. 29, 1997, p. 13.
77 According to *China News*, Dec. 1 1997, p. 2, the KMT candidate, Chen Ken-teh, spent TWD 1 billion and Annette Lu (DPP) TWD 300 million on the election campaign.
78 Cf *China News*, Nov. 26, 1997, p. 12.
79 Cf *Tai Wan Shi Bao*, Nov. 30, 1997, p. 7.
80 Cf '*Gong Bao*' for Tainan city in the November 29 elections 1997.
81 Cf *Tai Wan Shi Bao*, Nov. 30, 1997, p. 7.
82 Cf *TVBS Zhou Kan*, special election edition, Nov. 1997, p. 83.
83 Cf *United Daily*, Nov. 30, 1997, p. 6 and *TVBS Zhou Kan*, special election ed., Nov. 1997.
84 Taipei county is the largest constituency and comprehends a sufficient number of large cities to be compared with each other.
85 Cf *The China Post*, Nov. 11, 1997.
86 Another eligibility condition for old-age benefit is having worked five years in physically hard working conditions (classified by the central authority) and being more than 55 years old.
87 Cf *Min Zhong Shi Wan Bao*, Nov. 7, 1997.
88 'Beef', thus, stood for the social welfare policies of candidates in the highly competitive December 5 elections; cf for example: *Lian He Bao*, Nov. 9, 1998, p. 15; *Min Zhong Shi Wan Bao*, Nov. 9, 1998, p. 5; *Lian He Bao*, Nov. 11, 1998, p. 2; *Zi You Ri Bao*, Nov. 11, 1998, p. 4.
89 Cf *Zhong Yang Ri Bao News*, Dec. 6, 1998, p. 5.
90 Cf *Zhong Yang Ri Bao News*, Dec. 6, 1998, p. 5.
91 Cf *Zhong Yang Ri Bao News*, Dec. 6, 1998, p. 5 and p. 9; and *Lian He Bao*, Dec. 6, 1998, p. 1; own calculations.
92 Interviews with Chen Chu, Head of the Dept. of Social Welfare, Taipei City Government, April and May 1997.
93 Cf *Lian He Wan Bao*, Nov. 8, 1998, p. 1.
94 Cf *Lian He Bao*, Dec. 6, 1998, p. 1.
95 Cf *The China Post*, Nov. 6, 1997.
96 Cf *The China Post*, Nov. 6, 1997.
97 *Lian He Wan Bao*, Nov. 8, 1998, p. 1; *Min Zhong Shi Wan Bao*, Nov. 9, 1998, p. 5; and *Lian He Bao*, Nov. 9, 1998, p. 3.
98 Cf *Lian He Bao*, ibid.
99 Chen was a high profile serial murderer, kidnapper and rapist who shocked the population throughout 1997.
100 That is, the kidnapping of the family of the South African Ambassador. Hsieh had been instrumental in their release. Furthermore, it needs to be noted that, due to Hsieh's heavy presence in the media during the kidnapping of the family of the South African Ambassador, Hsieh's political career seemed to have been boosted more than ever before.
101 When he entered the house of the Ambassador, where the kidnapping took place, as a negotiator.
102 Cf *Min Zhong Shi Wan Bao*, Nov. 10, 1998, p. 8.
103 Ibid.
104 Cf *Lian He Bao*, Nov. 11, 1998, p. 3.

105 Cf *The Zi You Ri Bao*, Nov. 11, 1998, p. 4.
106 Cf *Lian He Bao*, Nov. 11, 1998, p. 2.
107 Cf Dong Zhe-sen (1998), *Lu Bian Mao Zhe Zheng Tuan*, p. 139.
108 Cf e.g. Ma Ying-jiou Jing Xuan Fu U Chu (1998), *Ma Ying-jiou Xing Dong Bai Pi Shu, She Hui Fu Li Pian.*
109 *Lian He Bao*, Dec. 6, 1998, p. 11.
110 For dates of party formations cf Ministry of Interior (1998), *Zheng Dang Ming Ce, Biao 4 - 24 B.*
111 Cf Central Election Commission (1998), *Di Xe Jie Li Fa Wei Yuan Xuan Ju Gai Kuang*, p. 36.
112 A particular feature of the SNTV system is the division into election districts which all have their own story, i.e. special competitive situations and factors determining the particular voting behavior of its constituents; for this reason the plural form 'elections' is used.
113 Calculated from Central Election Commission (1995), *Di San Jie Li Fa Wei Yuan Xuan Ju Gai Kuang*, p. 43.
114 Ibid, pp. 36, 68-9, 71-2.
115 In Taiwan, there are two special constituencies for aborigines, which overlap other electoral districts, i.e. one for low-land aborigines and one for high-land aborigines. In the Legislative Yuan, there are four seats reserved for each of the aborigine constituencies.
116 Cf Central Election Commission (1995), *Di San Jie Li Fa Wei Yuan Xuan Ju Gai Kuang*, Dec. 2, 1995; and *Lian He Bao*, Dec. 6, 1998, p. 1.
117 *Lian He Bao*, ibid, p. 1.
118 Cf *TVBS Zhou Kan*, No. 56, p. 22.
119 The Single Non-Transferable Vote system, SNTV.
120 The sub-group of proponents of vague (non-concrete) welfare statements has not been divided further because they appeared largely in short listings.
121 This is mainly the outcome of long term social changes, such as demographic changes, rising popularity of the nuclear family model, and rising female labor force participation (which causes a decline of unpaid care provision for the elderly inside the family).
122 Candidates proposed either the reform of the premium rate or an overall reform of national health insurance system.
123 Data are taken from the authors content analyses of public election circulars; taking the 25 largest constituencies each of which are over 100,000 valid votes; GINI coefficients are calculated after the formula: GINI = (1/2-B)/(1/2) = 1 - 2B where B is the area under the Lorenz curve; $B = (1/N)\ i(Y_{cum} - Y_i/2)$; N = number of candidates per constituency; Y_i = votes per candidates, Y_{cum} = cumulative votes per candidate; H = high, M = moderate, L = low.
124 Measuring the distribution of votes per candidates in each constituency.
125 In the SNTV system, each candidate represents one party. Thus, even candidates of one political party compete for votes. Therefore, we have decided to analyze the distribution of votes between candidates, and not parties.
126 Depending on the relative share of national seats, SNTV elections are *relatively unproportional*. Only *in the end (i.e. on an average)*, does the SNTV system result in a more or less similar distribution of votes *and* seats per party.
127 The distribution of national seats has a calming effect on electoral competition as candidates are not directly elected and can rely on the overall achievement of all other (directly elected) candidates of their party. However, this element is rather weak.
128 Martin Harrop and William L. Miller (1987), *Election and Voters*, p. 50.

129 Competitors who are not famous (i.e. candidates with only a few hundred votes) are not real competitors. Thus, the evenness of each candidates strength to attract votes influences electoral competition.

130 Cf e.g. Hubert M. Blalock (1979), *Social Statistics*, p. 84.

131 Coefficient of variation (=standard deviation/mean); *Category 1 include*s all candidates with three and more concrete welfare proposals, *Category 2* candidates with one or two concrete welfare proposals, *Category 3* candidates that promote the idea of social welfare but who are lacking concrete proposals, *Category 4* candidates who did not promote the idea of social welfare; data are taken from the election programs in the election circulars, the '*Gong Bao*', cf Central Election Commission (1998), *Di Se Jie Li Fa Wei Yuan Ju Gai Kuang*. The election programs are printed by each county and city government. Candidate number 3 in Hsinchu city, who withdraw from the election later on, was included as her election program was printed in the public '*Gong Bao*' as well.

132 = Index of the coefficient of variation, bases = overall coefficient of variation.

133 Indices of the coefficient of variation from 0 to 80 are classified as significantly lower, 80 to 90 as lower, 90 to 99 and 101 to 110 as similar, 100 as same, 110 to 120 as higher, 120 upwards as significantly higher.

134 Sign. = significant.

135 Measured by coefficient of variation of each constituency; data are results from the author's content analysis of 397 election programs in the public election circulars (i.e. '*Gong Bao*'), cf Table 7.

136 Which was able to extend its electorate continuously.

Appendices

Appendix 1: DPP Chairpersons from 1987 to 2000

Name	*Period*	***Affiliation to faction/group***
Jiang Peng-jian	1986-11-10 to 1987-11-10	lawyer defending Formosa prisoners
Yao Chia-wen	1987-11-10 to 1988-10-29	affiliated with New Tide faction*
Huang Hsin-chien	1988-10-29 to 1988-10-29	founder of Formosa faction
Huang Hsin-chien	1999-10-29 to 1991-10-13	founder of Formosa faction
Hsu Hsin-liang	1991-10-13 to 1994-05-01	founding member of Formosa faction
Shi Ming-teh	1994-05-01 to 1996-06-15	affiliated with New Tide faction*
Hsu Hsin-liang	1996-06-15 to 1998-06-07	founding member of Formosa faction
Lin Yi-hsiung	1998-06-07 to 2000-07-22	affiliated with New Tide faction*
Frank Hsieh	2000-07-22 to present	lawyer defending Formosa prisoners; and founder of Welfare State faction

Note: * former founding member of Formosa faction.
Source: www.dpp.org.tw (2000).

Appendix 2: KMT Chairpersons

Name	*Period*	*Place of birth*
Sun Yat-sen	1911 - 1925	Mainland China
Chiang Kai-shek	1926 - 1975	Mainland China
Chiang Ching-kuo	1975 - 1988	Mainland China
Lee Teng-hui	1988 - 2000	Taiwan
Lien Chan	2000 – to present	Mainland China

Appendix 3: DPP Survey Showing the Degree of Satisfaction of Voters, by sex, age group, and area

	Democratic Progressive Party		Kuomintang		New Party	
	satisfied	*not satisfied*	*satisfied*	*not satisfied*	*satisfied*	*not satisfied*
Total	*31.9 %*	*30,2 %*	*28.3 %*	*36.4 %*	*22.3 %*	*24.9 %*
Male (N=568)	35.9 %	36.2 %	30.6 %	**44.3 %**	27.9 %	30.8 %
Female (N=541)	27.8 %	23.7 %	26.2 %	28.2 %	26.1 %	19.0 %
20-29 years (N=283)	**42.6 %**	30.3 %	29.2 %	**45.2 %**	26.4 %	27.2 %
30-39 years (N=295)	**34.9 %**	34.7 %	26.5 %	**43.6 %**	24.0 %	26.6 %
40-49 years (N=216)	34.6 %	**31.3 %**	28.8 %	**38.7 %**	22.2 %	29.2 %
50-59 years (N=128)	22.1 %	**30.0 %**	**26.6 %**	**27.6 %**	18.2 %	24.2 %
60-69 years (N=107)	16.1 %	**21.1 %**	**28.0 %**	18.7 %	14.2 %	18.4 %
70+ years (N=75)	14.2 %	**21.2 %**	**36.8 %**	11.8 %	16.5 %	11.8 %
Urban area (N=586)	30.7 %	33.5 %	27.5 %	**40.7 %**	21.5 %	28.4 %
Rural area (N=486)	33.3 %	26.2 %	29.2 %	31.3 %	23.2 %	20.6 %

Source: www.dpp.org.tw (2000).

Appendix 4: Social Insurance Legislation

1950	Taiwan Province Labor Insurance Plan and Enforcement Regulations (implemented the same year)	
1950	Servicemen Insurance Plan (implemented the same year)	
1951	Taiwan Province Occupational Labor Insurance Plan	
1953	Fishermen's Insurance Plan (implemented the same year)	
1953	Insurance Provisions for Army, Navy, and Air Force Servicemen	1956
1958	Government Employee's Insurance Law	1974
1958	Labor Insurance Law	1968, 1973, 1979, 1988
1961	Regulations for Health Insurance of Government Employees	1985
1964	Insurance Plan for Retired Government Employees	1964, 1975
1970	Servicemen Insurance Provisions	
1975	Comprehensive Safety Insurance for Students in the Taiwan Province	1979, 1980
1980	Insurance Provisions for Teachers and Employees of Private Schools	
1980	Insurance Law for Senior Citizens	
1980	Insurance Law for the Disabled	1990
1982	Health Insurance Plan for Family Members of Government Employees	
1982	The Taiwan Providence Student's Comprehensive Accident Insurance Provisions	1990
1985	Health Insurance for Retired Government Employees	1988, 1990
1985	Health Insurance for Spouses of Retired Government Employees	1988, 1990
1985	Health Insurance for Spouses of Retired Private School Teachers and Employees	
1985	Temporary Provisions for Farmers' Insurance	
1989	Farmers' Health Insurance	
1989	Temporary Provisions for the Health Insurance for Local Representatives, Heads of Villages, Li and Lin, at all Levels of Provincial Government (The same regulations also apply to the municipalities of Taipei and Kaohsiung)	
1989	Health Insurance for Family Members of Teachers and Employees of Private Schools	1992
1991	Health Insurance for the Disabled and Handicapped	
1994	National Health Insurance Law (adapting the Government Employee's Insurance Law and the Labor Insurance Law)	

Sources: Chan and Yang (2001); CEPD (1996); W.I. Lin (1995), p. 219.

Appendix 5: Social Welfare Laws and Regulations

1943	Social Relief Law	
1965	Law of Financial Revenue and Expenses (Establishment of Social Welfare Fund)	1981 (Termination of SW Fund)
1972	The Regulation of Funds for Vocational Training	
1973	Children's Welfare Law	1993
1974	Law for Labor Security and Health	
1975	The Regulation of Public Housing	
1980	Social Assistance Law	
1980	Senior Citizens' Welfare Law	1993
1980	Welfare Law for the Disabled and Handicapped	1990
1989	Youth Welfare Law	
1990	Temporary Provisions for Low-Income Family Health Assistance	1992
1991	Welfare Law for the Handicapped and Disabled (providing social assistance in the fields of health, income and education)	

Sources: Chan and Yang (2001); Ku (1995); P.H. Lin (1996).

Appendix 6: Labor Welfare Laws and Regulations

1928	The Settlement of Labor Disputes Law
1929	Labor Union Law
1929	Factory Law
1931	Labor Inspection Law
1932	Collective Agreement Law
1936	Labor Contract Law
1943	Employee Welfare Fund Law
1943	Employee Welfare Fund Law Enforcement Rules
1972	The Regulation of Funds for Vocational Training
1974	Labor Safety and Health Law
1983	Rules Governing the Application of Foreign Nationals or Overseas Chinese Domiciled in Foreign Countries by Public or Private Enterprises in the ROC
1983	Vocational Training Act
1984	Labor Standards Law
1985	Enforcement Rules for the Labor Standards Law
1985	Rules for Setting Basic Wages
1985	Rules for Allocation & Management of Workers' Retirement Fund
1985	Rules on Leave-taking by Workers
1992	Employment Services Act

Note: without social insurance legislation.
Sources: GIO (1993); Ku (1995); and CLA (1997).

Appendix 7: The Administration of Social Welfare in the 1990s, by Governmental Authorities

Insurance for Military Servicemen	Ministry of Defense (& Central Trust of China)
Insurance for Government Employees	Ministry of Examination (& Central Trust of China)
Labor Insurance and Welfare	Council of Labor Affairs
Farmers Health Insurance	Council of Agriculture
Farmers Annuity	Council of Agriculture
Social Aid	Ministry of Interior, Dept. of Social Affairs
Social Workers	Ministry of Interior, Dept. of Social Affairs
Community Development	Ministry of Interior, Dept. of Social Affairs
Children's Welfare	Ministry of Interior, Dept. of Social Affairs
Women's Welfare	Ministry of Interior, Dept. of Social Affairs
Senior Citizens' Welfare	Ministry of Interior, Dept. of Social Affairs
Housing	Department of Housing
National Health Insurance	Department of Health
Unemployment Insurance	Council of Labor Affairs
National Pension Insurance	(Planning by Ministry of Economic Affairs, Council of Economic Planning and Development)

Sources: based on Chan and Yang (2001); and Ku (1995).

Appendix 8: An Overview of the Taiwanese Social Insurance System

	Insurance for Laborers	Insurance for Military	Insurance for Civil Servants	Insurance for Farmers	National Health Insurance
Time it went into operation	March 1950	June 1950	September 1958	October 1985	March 1995
Legislation it is based on	Labor Insurance Regulations	Military Servicemen Insurance Regulations	Gov't Employee Insurance Law	Farmers' Health Insurance Regulations	National Health Insurance Law
Adminis-trative unit	Council of Labor Affairs	Ministry of Defense	Ministry of Finance	Ministry of Interior and local governments	Department of Health
Adminis-trative sub-unit	Labor Insurance Bureau	Central Trust of China	Central Trust of China	Labor Insurance Bureaus	Health Insurance Bureau
Benefits granted for	disability, old age, death and unemploy-ment	disability, old age, and death	disability, old age, death and dependants' death	disability, and death	medical care for birth, sickness and injury

Source: based on Chang Bo-fei (1998), 'San Ji Nian Jin Zui Shang Pei Zhi Bi Li Yan Jiou', p. 37.

Appendix 9: The Distribution of Cash and Medical Benefits of the Farmers' Health Insurance Scheme in the First Years of Democratization (1986-1991)

	Total		Cash Benefit Payments		Medical Benefit Payments	
	mill. cases	mill. NTD	mill. cases	mill. NTD	mill. cases	mill. NTD
1986	1.1	0.9	0.003	0.074	1.1	0.8
1987	1.5	1.1	0.003	0.085	1.5	1.0
1987	3.4	2.3	0.005	0.184	3.4	2.2
1988	11.3	8.5	0.016	1.402	11.3	7.1
1989	22.1	18.2	0.034	4.380	22.1	13.8
1990	27.0	21.6	0.045	4.956	27.0	16.7
1991	34.1	27.4	0.047	5.106	34.1	22.2

Source: calculated from Department of Statistics, Ministry of Interior, (1993) 'Interior Statistics Monthly', pp. 32-3.

Appendix 10: Distribution of Different Benefits under the Farmers' Health Insurance Benefits (million NTD)

Year	Grand Total	Total Cash Bene-fits	Mater-nity Bene-fits	Dis-ability Bene-fits	Funeral Bene-fits	Total Medical Benefits	Inpatient Benefits	Outpatient Benefits
1985	90	6	1	-	4	84	55	28
1986	911	74	14	-	60	836	536	300
1987	1,146	85	15	-	70	1,060	640	420
1988	2,385	184	17	-	166	2,200	1,721	929
1989	8,582	1,403	40	5	1,357	7,178	4,083	3,094
1990	18,212	4,380	146	64	4,169	13,832	7,289	6,542
1991	21,664	4,956	307	85	4,564	16,707	8,028	8,679
1992	27,395	5,106	344	97	4,665	22,288	11,067	11,221
1993	29,574	5,290	382	98	4,809	24,283	10,336	13,947
1994	32,941	5,440	409	115	4,916	27,500	11,000	16,499
1995	12,087	5,611	200	251	6,159	6,475	2,972	3,500
1996	6,057	6,061	129	553	5,377	-3	-3	-1

Source: Bureau of Labor Insurance (1996), 'Yearbook of Labor Insurance Statistics, Republic of China', pp. 300-3.

Appendix 11: Display of Insurance Classes, Due Premiums and the Income Brackets Used for Calculating National Health Insurance Premiums

Insurance class	Income brackets	Basis for calculating premium	Monthly income
Class 1 with a premium of 600 NT	1	14,010	up to 14,010
	2	14,400	14,011-14,400
	3	15,000	14,401-15,000
	4	15,600	15,001-15,600
Class 2 with a premium of 900 NT	5	16,500	15,601-16,500
	6	17,400	16,501-17,400
	7	18,300	17,401-18,300
	8	19,200	18,301-19,200
	9	20,100	19,201-20,100
	10	21,000	20,101-21,000
	11	21,900	21,001-21,900
	12	22,800	21,901-22,800
Class 3 with a premium of 1,200 NT	13	24,000	22,801-24,200
	14	25,200	24,001-25,200
	15	26,400	25,201-27,600
	16	17,600	26,401-27,600
	17	28,800	27,601-28,800
Class 4 with a premium of 1,500 NT	18	30,300	28,801-24,000
	19	31,800	30,301-31,800
	20	33.300	31,801-33,300
	21	34,800	33,301-34,800
	22	36,300	34,801-36,300
Class 5 with a premium of 1,900 NT	23	38,200	36,301-38,200
	24	40,100	38,201-40,100
	25	42,000	40,101-42,000
	26	43,900	42,001-43,900
	27	45,800	43,901-45,800
Class 6 with a premium of 2,400 NT	28	48,200	45,801-48,200
	29	50,600	48,201-50,600
	30	53,000	50,601 and over

Source: Y.E. Chen (1995), 'Lao Gong Yu Chuan Min Jian Kang Bao Xuan Xi Lie Tan'.

Appendix 12: Comparison of Income Distribution in Taiwan and Other Countries

Countries	Year	Share of income by groups of Lowest 20 %	Share of income by groups of Highest 20 %	Ratio of income share of highest 20 % to that of lowest 20 % households	GINI concen-tration coefficient
Republic of China	1980	8.82	36.80	**4.17**	**0.2771**
	1988	7.89	38.25	**4.85**	**0.3030**
	1997	7.24	39.14	5.41	0.3199
South Korea	1993	7.47	39.29	5.26	0.2945
Hong Kong	1996	50.2	44.98	8.96	0.3736
Singapore	1992/3	5.70	48.23	8.46	0.3874
Japan	1994	8.07	38.03	**4.71**	**0.2789**
USA	1996	5.10	44.60	8.75	0.3660
Canada	1987	5.70	40.20	7.05	0.3272
U.K.	1988	4.60	44.30	9.63	0.3748
Sweden	1981	8.00	36.90	**4.61**	**0.2764**
Holland	1988	8.20	36.90	**4.50**	**0.2720**
Spain	1988	8.30	36.60	**4.41**	**0.2649**
Germany	1988	7.00	40.30	5.76	0.3145
France	1989	5.60	41.90	7.48	0.3372
China	1995	5.50	47.50	8.64	0.3860
Chile	1994	3.50	61.00	*17.43*	*0.5055*
Brazil	1989	2.10	67.50	*32.14*	*0.5697*

Note: GINI Indices for Mainland China, Chile and Brazil are calculated from income quintile grouped data< the GINI coefficients for the ROC is derived from disposable income of the ungrouped sample households.

Sources: World Development Report, 1997, The World Bank; Social Statistics Survey, South Korea, 1996; National Survey of Family Income and Expenditure, Japan, 1994; Income, Poverty and Evaluation of Noncash Benefits, USA, 1996; Population Census Main Report, Hong Kong, 1996; and Household Expenditure Survey, Singapore, 1996; quoted in DGBAS (1997b), 'Report of the Survey of Family Income and Expenditure in Taiwan Area of the Republic of China', p. 24.

Appendix 13: International Comparison of Unemployment Insurance Schemes

County	Benefits (in percent of salary)	Duration
Republic of China	50%	3 months to 16 months
USA	50%	26 weeks on an average (of all federal states)
United Kingdom	Every week 46.45 GBP	52 weeks
South Korea	50%	60-210 days depending on contributions and age
Japan	60-80% (depending on income level)	90-300 days depending on contributions, age and work prospects
Austria	40-50%	20-30 weeks
Belgium	60% (40% after one year)	At least 18 months
Canada	55%	50 weeks
France	57.4%	4-20 months depending on age and contributions
Greece	40%	12 months
Italy	20-80%	180 days
Germany	68% (63% for single persons)	78-832 days
Luxembourg	80% (after 6 months gradually decreasing to 64%)	12 months
Holland	70%	6-36 months depending on age and work record
Norway	62%	19 months
Spain	70% (40% after 6 months)	24 months depending on contributions

Source: Social Security Programs Throughout the World, 1993, quoted in Council of Labor Affairs (1999), 'Lao Gong Bao Xuan She Ye Gei Fu Shuo Tie'.

References

Arrigo, Linda Gail (1994), From Democratic Movement to Bourgeois Democracy: The Internal Politics of the Taiwan Democratic Progress Party in 1991, in Murry A. Rubinstein (ed.), *The Other Taiwan: 1945 to the Present*, M.E. Sharpe: New York.

Arrigo, Linda Gail (2000), An Old-time Politician who Stepped Forward, *Taipei Times*, February 11.

Aspalter, Christian (2001a), *Conservative Welfare State Systems in East Asia*, Praeger: Westport, CT.

Aspalter, Christian (2001b), *Importance of Christian and Social Democratic Movements in Welfare Politics*, Nova Science: New York.

Aspalter, Christian (2001c), Südkorea und Taiwan: Eine Neue Ära der Konservativen Sozialpolitik, in Johannes Jäger *et al.* (eds), *Sozialpolitik in der Peripherie*, Brandes & Apsel / Südwind: Frankfurt a.M., Germany.

Aspalter, Christian (2001d), The Taiwanese Economic Miracle: From Sugar Cane to High-Technology, in C. Aspalter (ed.), *Understanding Modern Taiwan, Essays in Economics, Politics and Social Policy*, Ashgate: Aldershot.

Aspalter, Christian (2002), Discovering Old and New Shores in Welfare State Theory, in C. Aspalter (ed.), *Discovering the Welfare State in East Asia*, Praeger: Westport, CT.

Bai, Hsiu-hsiung (1979), *She Hui Fu Li Xing Zheng*, San Min Shu Ju: Taipei.

Bai, Hsiu-hsiung (1980), *Rui Dian Mei Guo Ji Wo Guo She Hui Fu Li Bi Jiao Yan Jiou*, Zhong Guo She Hui Fu Li Xie Jin Hui: Taipei.

Baldwin, Peter (1990), *The Politics of Social Solidarity: The Class Bases of the European Welfare State*, Cambridge University Press: Cambridge.

Bartolini, Stefano (1995), Parteienkonkurrenz, in B. Nedelmann (ed.), *Politische Institutionen im Wandel*, Westdeutscher Verlag: Opladen.

Beetham, David (1985), *Max Weber and the Theory of Modern Politics*, Polity Press: Cambridge.

BNHI, Bureau of National Health Insurance (1998), *National Health Insurance Annual Statistical Report*, BNHI: Taipei.

Blalock, Hubert M. (1979), *Social Statistics*, Mc Graw-Hill: New York.

BLI, Bureau of Labor Insurance, ROC (1997), *Yearbook of Labor Insurance Statistics, Republic of China*, Taipei.

BLI, Bureau of Labor Insurance, ROC (1999), *Lau Gong Bao Xuan She Ye Gei Fu Shen Jing Zhen Zhi*, Taipei.

Bosco, Joseph (1994), Taiwan Factions: Guanxi, Patronage, and the State of Local Politics, in Rubinstein, Murray A. (ed.), *The Other Taiwan: 1945 to the Present*, M.E. Sharpe: New York.

Bottomore, Tom (1964, 1993), *Élites and Society*, Routledge: London.

Budge, Ian and Keman, Hans (1990), *Parties and Democracies, Coalition Formation and Government Functioning in Twenty States*, Oxford University Press: London.

Castles, Francis G. (1985b), *The Working Class and Welfare*, Allen & Unwin: Wellington.

Central Election Commission, MOI (1995), *Di San Jie Li Fa Wei Yuan Xuan Ju Gai Kuang*, Taipei.

Central Election Commission, MOI (1998), *Di Se Jie Li Fa Wei Yuan Xuan Ju Gai Kuang*, Taipei.

CEPD, Council for Economic Planning and Development (1996), *She Hui Fu Li Zhi Zhu Dui Cong Ti Jing Ji Fa Zhan Zhi Ying Xiang*, CEPD: Taipei.

Chan, Hou-sheng Gordon (1985), Taiwan, in J. Dixon and H.S. Kim (eds), *Social Welfare in Asia*, Crom Helm: Beckenham.

Chan, Hou-sheng and Xu, Ron-zong (1991), Wo Men De She Hui Wen Ti Zai Na Li, in H.S. Chan (ed.), *She Hui Bian Qian Yu She Hui Fu Li*, Tsai Tuan Fa Ren Min Zhu Wen Jiao Ji Jin Hui: Taipei.

Chan, Hou-sheng and Yang, Ying (2001), The Development of Social Welfare in Taiwan, in C. Aspalter (ed.), *Understanding Modern Taiwan, Essays in Economics, Politics and Social Policy*, Ashgate: Aldershot.

Chan, Lian (1994), Innovation through Pragmatism, in Jason C. Hu (ed.), *Taiwan's Quiet Revolution*, Kwang Hwa: Taipei.

Chan, Yi-zhang (1997), You Fong Xian Guan Dian Tan Tao Lao Nian Jing Ji An Chuan Yu Bao Zhang, *She Hui Zheng Ce Yu She Hui Gong Zuo Xue Kan*, Journal of Social Policy and Social Work, Vol. 1, No. 2, pp. 3-38.

Chang, Bo-fei (1998), *San Ji Nian Jin Zui Shang Pei Zhi Bi Li Yan Jiou*, thesis, National Taiwan University, Taipei.

Chang, Parris H. (1992), The Changing Nature of Taiwan's Politics, in Dennis F. Simon and Michael Y.M. Kau (eds), *Taiwan: Beyond the Economic Miracle*, M.E. Sharpe: New York.

Chen, Cheng (1961), *Land Reform in Taiwan*, China Publishing: Taipei.

Chen, Hsiao-hung Nancy (2000), *Searching for Social Insurance Model(s): Taiwan's National Pension System in the Making*, research paper, Department of Sociology, National Chengchi University: Taipei.

Chen, L.T. (1990), Bibliographical Sketch of Dr. Sun Yat-sen, printed in Shaw Yu-ming (ed.), *The Three Principles of the People*, Government Information Office, Republic of China: Taipei, pp. iv-ix.

Chen, Sung-shan (2001), New Tide Rising in DPP Signals a Change, *Taipei Times*, April 12.

Chen, Wu-hsiung (1996), Wo Guo Lao Ren Fu Li Zheng Ce De Xian Xing Zuo Fang Yu Wei Lai Chan Wang, *Community Development Journal*, Vol. 74.

Chen, Y.E. (1995), Lao Gong Yu Chuan Min Jian Kang Bao Xuan Xi Lie Tan, *Taiwan Laogong*, No. 30.

Cheng, Tun-jen and Hsu, Yung-ming (1996), Issue Structure, the DPP's Factionalism, and Party Realignment, in Tien Hung-mao (ed.), *Taiwan's Electoral Politics and Democratic Transition: Riding the Third Wave*, M.E. Sharpe: New York.

China News (1997), Nov. 1, 4, 8, 15, 24, 25, 26, 27, 29, 30, and Dec. 1, 9.

Chow, Nelson W.S. and Xu, Yuebin (2001), *Socialist Welfare in a Market Economy*, Ashgate: Aldershot.

Chu, Yun-han and Lin, Tse-min (1996), The Process of Democratic Consolidation in Taiwan: Social Cleavage, Electoral Competition, and the Emerging Party System, in Tien Hung-mao (ed.), *Taiwan's Electoral Politics and Democratic Transition: Riding the Third Wave*, M.E. Sharpe: New York.

CLA, Council of Labor Affairs (1997), *Lao Gong Fa Gui Ji Yao*, Taipei, Council of Labor Affairs, ROC, January.

CLA, Council of Labor Affairs (1999), *Lao Gong Bao Xuan She Ye Gei Fu Shuo Tie*, Council of Labor Affairs, ROC, January.

Clarke, Cal (1989), *Taiwan's Development: Implications for Contending Political Economy Paradigms*, Greenwood: Westport, CT.

Collier, David and Messick, Richard E. (1975), Prerequisites Versus Diffusion: Testing Alternative Explanations of Social Security Adaption, *American Political Science Review*, Vol. 69, pp. 1299-1315.

Constitution of the Republic of China (1947), ROC.

Copper, John F. (1981a), Taiwan's Recent Election: Progress Toward a Democratic System, in James C. Hsiung, *et al.* (eds), *Contemporary Republic of China: The Taiwan Experience 1950 to 1980*, Praeger: New York.

Copper, John F. (1981b), Political Development in Taiwan, in James C. Hsiung *et al.* (eds), *Contemporary Republic of China: The Taiwan Experience 1950 to 1980*, Praeger: New York.

Copper, John F. (1990), *Taiwan: Nation-State or Province*, Westview Press: Boulder.

Copper, John F. (1992), *China Diplomacy: The Washington-Taipei-Beijing Triangle*, Westview: Boulder.

Copper, John F. (1998), *Taiwan's Mid-1990s Elections: Taking the Final Steps to Democracy*, Greenwood: Westport, CT.

CTC, Central Trust of China, ROC (1997), *Statistical Data for Government Employees' Insurance*, Republic of China, Taipei.

DGBAS, Directorate-General for Budget, Accounting and Statistics (1996), *Social Indicators 1995*, DGBAS: Taipei

DGBAS, Directorate-General of Budget, Accounting and Statistics (1997a), *Yearbook of Manpower Survey Statistics*, DGBAS: Taipei.

DGBAS, Directorate-General of Budget, Accounting and Statistics (1997b), *Report of the Survey of Family Income and Expenditure in Taiwan Area of the Republic of China*, DGBAS, Executive Yuan.

Dickson, Bruce J. (1996), The Kuomintang Before Democratization: Organizational Change and the Role of Elections, in Tien Hung-mao (ed.), *Taiwan's Electoral Politics and Democratic Transition: Riding the Third Wave*, M.E. Sharpe: New York.

Dixon, John E. (1995), *Social Security and the Ghosts that Haunt It*, in J.E. Dixon and R.P. Scheurell (eds), *Social Security Programs: A Cross-Cultural Comparative Perspective*, Greenwood Press: Westport, CT.

Dixon, John E. (1998), An Exploration of Emerging Global Trends in Social Security, in S. MacPherson and H.K. Wong (eds), *Social Development in Societies in Transition*, Ashgate: Aldershot.

Dong, Zhe-sen (1998), *Lu Bian Mao Zhe Zheng Tuan*, Er Neng Publishing Co: Taipei.

Downs, Anthony (1968), *Ökonomische Theorie der Demokratie*, Mohr: Tübingen.

Esping-Andersen, Gøsta (1985), *Politics Against Markets, The Social Democratic Road to Power*, Princeton University Press: Princeton.

Esping-Andersen, Gøsta (1990), *Three Worlds of Welfare Capitalism*, Polity Press: Cambridge.

Esping-Andersen, Gøsta (1999), *Social Foundations of Postindustrial Economies*, Oxford University Press: Oxford.

Eyton, Laurence (2000), Made in Taiwan, *Taipei Times*, March 16.

Fei, John C.H., Ranis, Gustav and Kuo, Shirley W.Y. (1979), *Growth with Equity: The Taiwan Case*, Oxford University Press: New York, 1979.

Ferrera, Maurizio (1993), *Modelli di Solidarietà, Politica e Riforme Sociali nelle Democrazie*, Il Mulino: Bologna, Italy.

Freedomhouse (1998), *Freedom in the World: The Annual Survey of Political Rights & Civil Liberties, 1997-1998*, Transactions: New Brunswick.

George, Vic (1973), *Social Security and Society*, Routledge and Kegan Paul: London.

GIO, Government Information Office, ROC (1993), *The Republic of China Yearbook 1993*, Taipei.

Glough, Ralph N. (1981), The Political System of Taiwan, in James C. Hsiung *et al.* (eds), *Contemporary Republic of China: The Taiwan Experience 1950 to 1980*, Praeger: New York.

Gold, Thomas B. (1986), *State and Society in the Taiwan Miracle*, East Gate Books: New York.

Habermas, Jürgen (1989), *Legitimationsprobleme im Spätkapitalismus*, Suhrkamp: Frankfurt.

Harrop, Martin and Miller, William L. (1987), *Election and Voters, A Comparative Introduction*, MacMillan: London.

Ho, Samuel P.S. (1978), *Economic Development in Taiwan, 1860-1970*, Yale University Press: New Haven.

Ho, Shuet Ying (1990), *Taiwan – After a Long Silence: The Emerging New Unions of Taiwan*, Asia Monitor Research Center: Hong Kong.

Hsiao, Michael H.H. (2001), Taiwan's Social Welfare Movement in the 1980s, in C. Aspalter (ed.), *Understanding Modern Taiwan, Essays in Economics, Politics and Social Policy*, Ashgate: Aldershot.

Hsu, Crystal (2001), Huang Chu-wen Faces Greatest Test, *Taipei Times*, July 2.

Hu, Fu and Chu, Yun-han (1992), Electoral Competition and Political Democratization, in T.C. Cheng and S. Haggard (eds), *Political Change in Taiwan*, Lynne Rienner Publ.: Boulder.

Huang, Joyce (2001a), Faction Leaders Slam New Tide, *Taipei Times*, April 4.

Huang, Joyce (2001b), DPP Holds Memorial for Fu Ceng, *Taipei Times*, May 10.

Huang, Song-lin (2000), *Domiciliary Care for the Elderly People Living Alone in Taiwan Province: An Analysis of Needs and Use of Services*, paper presented at SPA conference, University of Surrey-Roehampton, London.

Huang, Teh-fu (1996), Elections and the Evolution of the Kuomintang, in Hung-mao Tien (ed.), *Taiwan's Electoral Politics and Democratic Transition: Riding the Third Wave*, M.E. Sharpe: New York.

Hwang, Y.S. and Hill, M. (1997), The 1995 Health Reforms in Taiwan – An Analysis of the Policy Process, *Hong Kong Public Administration*, Vol. 6, No. 2, pp. 79-95.

Jacobs, Bruce (2000), Completing the Circle, *Taipei Times*, March 23.

Jacobs, Bruce (2001), Factions Determine Election Dealing, *Taipei Times*, Nov. 28.

Janoski, Thomas (1998), *Citizenship and Civil Society*, Cambridge University Press: Cambridge.

Jiang, Ping-lung and Wu, Wen-cheng (1992), The Changing Role of the KMT in Taiwan's Political System, in T.C. Cheng and S. Haggard (eds), *Political Change in Taiwan*, Lynne Rienner Publ.: Boulder.

Korpi, Walter (1980), *The Working Class in Welfare Capitalism*, Routledge & Kegan Paul: London.

Korpi, Walter (1983), *The Democratic Class Struggle*, Routledge and Kegan Paul: London.

Ku, Yeun-wen (1995), *Welfare Capitalism in Taiwan, State, Economy and Social Policy*, MacMillan: London.

Ku, Yeun-wen (2002), Towards a Taiwanese Welfare State? Demographic Change, Politics and Social Policy, in C. Aspalter (ed.), *Discovering the Welfare State in East Asia*, Praeger: Westport, CT.

Kuo, Andy Yin-han (2000), *The Development of Social Assistance as an Issue of Central-local Relations in Taiwan: A Case Study of the Income Support for Elderly*, paper presented at the Social Policy Association annual conference, University of Surrey-Roehampton, London.

Kwon, Huck-ju (1998), Democracy and the Politics of Social Welfare: A Comparative Analysis of Welfare Systems in East Asia, in R. Goodman, G. White and H.J. Kwon (eds), *The East Asian Welfare Model*, Routledge: London.

Lai, Tse-han, Myers, Ramon H., and Wei, Wou (eds) (1991), *A Tragic Beginning, The Taiwan Uprising of February 28, 1947*, Stanford University Press: Stanford, CA.

Lao Gong Fa Gui Ji Yao, *Labor Insurance Act*, ROC.

Lee, Chang-kuei (2001), Taiwan Needs 'Nativization' Party, *Taipei Times*, July 15.

Legislative Yuan (1997), Handicapped Benefits, *Chinese Legislative News Review Series* (in Chinese), Vol. 60.

Lian He Bao (United Daily News) (1997), Nov. 30.

Lian He Bao (United Daily News) (1998), Nov. 9, Nov. 11, and Dec. 6.

Lian He Wan Bao (United Evening News) (1998), Nov. 8.

Liao, Feng-chen (1997), Nian Jin Huan Xuan Piao, You Piao?, *Global Views Monthly*, November.

Lin, Chieh-yu (2001), Stage Set for Coalition-Building, *Taipei Times*, Dec. 2.

Lin, Chieh-yu and Ide, William (2001), Lee on the Offensive at First TSU Rallies, *Taipei Times*, September 2.

Lin, Mei-chun (2001a), Lee Teng-hui Seeks KMT Legislators, *Taipei Times*, Dec. 28.

Lin, Mei-chun (2001b), Number Six – KMT Expels Lee, *Taipei Times*, Dec. 30.

Lin, Pei-hua (1996), *Tai Wan Lao Nian Fu Li Zheng Ce Yan Jin Zhi Zheng Zhi Jing Ji Fen Xi*, Dissertation, National Taiwan University: Taipei.

Lin, Tse-min and Zhang, Bao-hui (1998), Cross-cutting Issues and the Consolidation of Democracy in Taiwan, in P. Burnell and P. Calvert (eds), *Democratization*, Frank Cass: Ilford, UK.

Lin, Wan-I (1995), *Tai Wan De She Hui Fu Li: Min Qian Guan Dian*, Wu Nan Tu Shu: Taipei.

Local Election Commissions of each County and City Magistrate (1997), all *'Gong Bao'* (public circular containing information on elections, the candidates, and their election program) for the November 29 Elections.

Local Election Commissions of each County and City Magistrate (1998), all *'Gong Bao'* for the December 5 Elections.

Long, Simon (1991), *Taiwan: China's Last Frontier*, MacMillan: London.

Low, Stephanie (2001), KMT Breaks it off with Lee Teng-hui, *Taipei Times*, September, 22.

Lu, Hsiu-lien Annette (1997), *Zhong Shen Mei Li Dao*, Taiwan Wen She Books: Taipei.

Ma Ying-jiou Jing Xuan Fu U Chu (1998), *Ma Ying-jiou Xing Dong Bai Pi Shu, She Hui Fu Li Pian*, Taipei.

Marshall, T.H. (1964), *Class, Citizenship and Social Development*, The University of Chicago Press: Chicago.

Min Zhong Shi Wan Bao (The Commons Daily) (1997), Nov. 2, 7, 24, 30.

Min Zhong Shi Wan Bao (The Commons Daily) (1998), Nov. 9, 10.

ML, Martial Law, (1949), *Jie lan Fa*, Republic of China.

MOI, Department of Statistics, Ministry of Interior (1993), *Interior Statistics Monthly*, Ministry of Interior: Taipei, January.

MOI, Department of Statistics, Ministry of Interior (1998a), *Monthly Bulletin of Interior Statistics*, Ministry of Interior: Taipei, December.

MOI, Department of Statistics, Ministry of Interior (1998b), *Ben Shen She Li An Lao Ren An, Liao Yang Ji Gou Yi Lan Biao*, updated internal document, Ministry of Interior: Taipei.

MOI, Ministry of Interior, (1998c), *Zheng Dang Ming Ce, Biao 4 - 24 B*, October 7.

Moody, Peter R. (1992), *Political Change on Taiwan: A Study of Ruling Party Adaptability*, Praeger: New York.

Moore, Barrington Jr. (1967), *Social Origins of Dictatorship and Democracy: Lord and Peasant in the Making of the Modern World*, Beacon: Boston.

O'Connor, James (1973), *The Fiscal Crisis of the State*, St. Martins Press: New York.

Offe, Claus (1984a), *Arbeitsgesellschaft*, Campus: Frankfurt.

Offe, Claus (1984b), *Contradictions of the Welfare State* (ed. by J. Keane), MIT Press: Cambridge.

Olson, Mancur (1976), Die Logik des kollektiven Handelns, in W. Dettling (ed.), *Die Macht der Verbände*, Lozog: Munich.

Olson, Mancur (1982), *The Rise and Decline of Nations*, Yale University Press: New Haven.

Olson, Marvin E. (1970), Élitist Theory as a Response to Marx, in M.E. Olson (ed.), *Power in Societies*, MacMillan: London.

Peng, Ming-min (1972), *A Taste of Freedom: Memoirs of a Formosan Independence Leader*, Holt, Rinehart and Winston: New York.

Pierson, Paul (1995), *Dismantling the Welfare State?*, Cambridge University Press: Cambridge.

Ramesh, Mishra (1984), *The Welfare State in Crisis, Social Thought and Social Change*, Wheatsheaf: Brighton.

Rimlinger, Gaston V. (1971), *Welfare Policy and Industrialization in Europe, America and Russia*, John Wiley and Sons: New York.

Schafferer, Christian (2001), Liberalization and Democratization in Taiwan, in C. Aspalter (ed.), *Understanding Modern Taiwan*, Ashgate: Aldershot.

Shalev, Michael (1983a), Class Politics and the Western Welfare State, in S.E. Spiro (ed.), *Evaluating the Welfare State*, Academic Press: New York.

Shalev, Michael (1983b), The Social Democratic Model and Beyond: Two 'Generations' of Comparative Research on the Welfare State, *Comparative Social Research*, Vol. 6.

Skocpol, Theda (1987a), America's Incomplete Welfare State, in M. Rein, G. Esping-Andersen and L. Rainwater (eds), *Stagnation and Renewal in Social Policy*, M.E. Sharpe: New York.

Skocpol, Theda (1987b), A Society Without a 'State'? Political Organization, Social Conflict, and Welfare Provision in the United States, *Journal of Public Policy*, Vol. 7, No 4.

Skocpol, Theda (1992), *Protecting Soldiers and Mothers, The Political Origins of Social Policy in the United States*, Harvard University Press: Cambridge.

Soong, C.Y. James (1994), Political Development in the Republic of China on Taiwan, 1985-1992: An Insider's View, in Jason C. Hu (ed.), *Taiwan's Quiet Revolution*, Kwang Hwa: Taipei.

Stephens, John D. (1979), *The Transition from Capitalism to Socialism*, MacMillan: London.

Sun, Jian-zhong (1997), She Hui Jin Tie Shi Shi Jing Yan De Fan Xing: Yi Jing Lau Jin Tie Wei Li, *She Hui Zheng Ce Yu She Hui Gong Zuo Xue Kan*, Journal of Social Policy and Social Work, June, pp. 73-98

Sun, Yat-sen (1990), San Min Chu I, in Shaw Yu-ming (ed.), *The Three Principles of the People*, Government Information Office, Republic of China: Taipei, pp. 1-212.

Tai Wan Ri Bao (Taiwan Daily) (1997), Nov. 30.

Tai Wan Shi Bao (Taiwan Times) (1997), Nov. 30.

Taipei Municipal Government (1997), *The Statistical Abstract of Taipei Municipality*, Taipei Municipal Government: Taipei.

The China Post (1997), Nov. 1, 6, 7, 9, 11, 12, 28, and Dec. 1.

Thoenes, Piet (1970), The Élite in the Welfare State, in M.E. Olson (ed.), *Power in Societies*, MacMillan: London.

Tien, Hung-mao (1992), Taiwan's Evolution Toward Democracy: A Historical Perspective, in Dennis F. Simon and Michael Y.M Kau (eds), *Taiwan: Beyond the Economic Miracle*, M.E. Sharpe: New York.

Tien, Hung-mao (1996), Elections and Taiwan's Democratic Development, in Tien Hung-mao (ed.), *Taiwan's Electoral Politics and Democratic Transition: Riding the Third Wave*, M.E. Sharpe: New York.

Titmuss, Richard M. (1958), *Essays on 'the Welfare State'*, Allen & Unwin: London.

Titmuss, Richard M. (1974), *Social Policy*, Allen & Unwin: London.

Titmuss, Richard M. (1987), Developing Social Policy in Conditions of Rapid Change, in B. Abel-Smith and K. Titmuss (eds), *The Philosophy of Welfare: Selected Writings of Richard M. Titmuss*, Allen & Unwin: London.

Tocqueville, Alexis de (1980), The Social Origins of Democracy, in J. Stone and S. Mennell (eds), *Alexis de Tocqueville, On Democracy, Revolution and Society, Selected Writings*, The University of Chicago Press: Chicago.

TP, *Temporary Provisions Effective During the Period of Communist Rebellion* (1948, 1960, 1966), Republic of China.

Tsai Song-zhao (1989), *Lao Ren Fu Li Zheng Ce*, Gui Guan: Taipei.

Tsai Song-zhao (1990), *She Hui Fu Li Zheng Ce – Fu Li Yu Jing Ji De Zeng He*, Taipei.

TVBS Zhou Kan (TVBS weekly) (1997), special election edition, November.

TVBS Zhou Kan (TVBS weekly) (1997), Nov. 22, Dec. 6.

TVBS Zhou Kan (TVBS weekly) (1998), No. 56.

Tzou, Jiing-wen (2001), Former President Talks About Past and Future, *Taipei Times*, September 3.

Weir, Margaret, Orloff, Ann Shola, and Skocpol, Theda (1988), Introduction: Understanding American Social Politics, in M. Weir, A.S. Orloff, and T. Skocpol (eds), *The Politics of Social Policy in the United States*, Princeton University Press: Princeton.

Wilensky, H.L. and Lebeaux, C.N. (1958), *Industrial Society and Social Welfare*, Russell Sage Foundation: New York.

Wilensky, H.L. and Turner, L. (1987), *Democratic Corporatism and Policy Linkages*, Institute of International Studies, University of California: Berkeley.

Wilensky, Harold L. (1975), *The Welfare State and Equality: Structural and Ideological Roots of Public Expenditures*, University of California Press: Berkeley.

Wilensky, Harold L. (1981), Leftism, Catholicism, and Democratic Corporatism, in P. Flora and A. Heidenheimer (eds), *The Development of Welfare States in Europe and America*, Transaction: New Brunswick.

Wu, Jau-shieh Joseph (1995), *Taiwan's Democratization: Forces Behind the New Movement*, Oxford University Press: Oxford.

Xu, Jin-wen (1993), *Tai Wan Hai Xia Liang An Lao Ren Fu Li Zhi Bi Jiao Yan Jiou*, thesis, National Taiwan University: Taipei.

Xu, Li-zhong (1989), *Lao Ren Wen Ti Yu Tui Ce – Lao Ren Fu Li Fu U Zhi Tan Tao Yu She Ji*, Gui Guan: Taipei.

Yang, San-kuang (1992), *Cong Jia Ting Gong Neng Kan Wo Guo She Hui Fu Li Zheng Ce De Fa Zhan: Jia Ting Wei Zhong Xin De She Hui Fu Li Zheng Ce*, thesis, National Taiwan University: Taipei.

Ye, Su-ke (1996), *Welfare Configuration: The East Asian NICs and OECD Countries Compared*, dissertation, University of Tasmania.

Yeh, Lindy (2001), Voter Deal KMT a Second Blow, *Taipei Times*, Dec. 2.

Zhao, Sui-sheng (1996), *Power by Design: Constitution-making in Nationalist China*, University of Hawaii Press: Hawaii.

Zheng, Kuan-chen (1995), Tai Wan Di Qu De Ren Kou Bian Qian Yu She Hui An Chuan, *Community Development Journal*, No. 70, June.

Zhong Shi Wan Bao (China Times Express) (1997), Nov. 12 to 29.

Zhong Yang Ri Bao (Central Daily News) (1997), Nov. 2, 30.

Zhong Yang Ri Bao (Central Daily News) (1998), Dec. 6.

Zi Li Cao Bao (The Independence Morning Post) (1997), Nov. 30.

Zi You Ri Bao (The Liberty Times) (1997), Nov. 1, 2, 6, 7, 30.

Zi You Ri Bao (The Liberty Times) (1998), Nov. 11.

Quoted Interviews

CHC, Chen Chu (two interviews), then Head of the Department of Social Welfare, Taipei City Government, April/May 1997.

EXP, Social Welfare Department, Ministry of Interior, anonymous expert, Taipei, October, 1998.

LWI, Lin Wan-I, National Taiwan University, May, 1998.

SCH, Christian Schafferer, National Taiwan University, January, 2001.

TAO, Liu Tao, policy analyst, DPP Headquarters, Taipei, November, 1997.

Websites Frequently Used for Collecting Data

CEC, Central Election Commission, *www.cec.gov.tw*
DPP, *www.dpp.org.tw*
Election Studies Center, National Cheng Chi University, *www.esc.nccu.edu.tw*
GIO, Government Information Office, *www.gio.gov.tw*
Green Party, *www.greenparty.org.tw*
Ito, Kiyoshi (2000), Taiwan, 400 Years of History and Outlook, *www.leksu.com*
KMT, *www.kmt.org.tw*
Legislative Yuan, *www.ly.gov.tw*
National Assembly, *www.nasm.gov.tw*
New Party homepage, *www.np.org.tw*
People First Party homepage, *www.pfp.org.tw*
TAIP, Taiwan Independence Party, *www.taip.org.tw*
TSU, Taiwan Solidarity Union, *www.tsu.org.tw*
Taipei Times homepage, *www.taipeitimes.com/news*
University of Würzburg, collection of world's constitutions, *www.uni-wuerzburg.de/law*
YAM search engine, *www.yam.com*

Index